MASONIC

PARLIAMENTARY LAW.

MASONIC

PARLIAMENTARY LAW:

OR,

PARLIAMENTARY LAW APPLIED TO THE GOVERNMENT OF MASONIC BODIES.

A GUIDE FOR

THE TRANSACTION OF BUSINESS IN LODGES, CHAPTERS, COUNCILS, AND COMMANDERIES.

BY

ALBERT G. MACKEY, M.D.,

PAST GENERAL GRAND HIGH PRIEST, U. S. A.; AUTHOR OF THE "ENCYCLOPÆDIA OF FREEMASONRY," "MANUAL OF THE LODGE," "BOOK OF THE CHAPTER," ETC.

———

PHILADELPHIA:

MOSS & COMPANY,

432 CHESTNUT STREET,

1875.

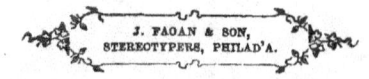

J. FAGAN & SON,
STEREOTYPERS, PHILAD'A.

PRINTED BY HENRY B. ASHMEAD, PHILADELPHIA.

TO

ROBERT FARMER BOWER, 33 ∴

PAST GRAND COMMANDER

AND

PAST GRAND HIGH PRIEST,

OF

IOWA,

𝕿𝖍𝖊 𝕬𝖚𝖙𝖍𝖔𝖗 𝕯𝖊𝖉𝖎𝖈𝖆𝖙𝖊𝖘 𝖙𝖍𝖎𝖘 𝖂𝖔𝖗𝖐,

AS

A MARK OF HIS ESTEEM,

AND AS

𝕬 𝕿𝖗𝖎𝖇𝖚𝖙𝖊 𝖔𝖋 𝖍𝖎𝖘 𝕱𝖗𝖎𝖊𝖓𝖉𝖘𝖍𝖎𝖕.

CONTENTS.

CHAPTER IX.

CHAPTER X.

CHAPTER XI.

CHAPTER XII.

CHAPTER XIII.

CHAPTER XIV.

CHAPTER XV.

CHAPTER XVI.

CHAPTER XVII.

CHAPTER XVIII.

CHAPTER XIX.

CHAPTER XX.

CHAPTER XXI.

CHAPTER XXII.

CHAPTER XXIII.

CHAPTER XXIV.

CHAPTER XXV.

CHAPTER XXVI.

CHAPTER XXVII.

CHAPTER XXVIII.

CHAPTER XXIX.

CHAPTER XXX.

CHAPTER XXXI.

CHAPTER XXXII.

PREFACE.

M R. WILSON, in his very able *Digest of Parliamentary Law*, has remarked that "it would be well for persons presiding at meetings of any description to make themselves familiar with the rules of Parliament in regard to questions and amendments which have been tested by long experience, and are found as simple and efficient in practice, as they are logical in principle."

Much experience in conducting the business of Masonic bodies, or in seeing it conducted by others, has convinced me that a treatise which should, in perspicuous language, prescribe the rules for the government of Lodges, Chapters, or any other assemblies of Masons in their Masonic character, could not fail, if properly executed, to be of service to the Craft.

It is evident that when one is, for the first time, called to preside over a Lodge of Freemasons, he must come to the performance of that important duty, either with no knowledge whatever of the rules of order that govern the proceedings of deliberative bodies, or with a familiarity with those rules only that are exclusively derived from the ordinary parliamentary law.

From either of these conditions, errors must inevitably arise. He who knows nothing of the rules which direct and govern deliberative bodies, will, when he takes the Oriental chair, find himself at an absolute loss to control a debate or to put a question. He who derives his knowledge from only the general principles of parliamentary law, will be continually committing errors by applying those principles, without modification, to the government of a Lodge.

The business of Masonic bodies must be conducted by established rules; but these rules differ in many respects from those which govern other assemblies. A proper text-book of Masonic parliamentary law should be one in which the law of Parliament should be given as it is modified by the higher law of Masonry; so that the presiding officer of a Lodge or Chapter may find in it the authority for his decisions on points of order, and a guide for the direction of his conduct in controlling the deliberations and discussions of the brethren over whom he has been placed.

Manuals of parliamentary law are not uncommon. But unless they are accompanied by those modifications which make them applicable to Masonic law, they are not only useless, but productive of error to the Mason who takes them for his guide.

A book which should point out the essential differences between the ordinary law of Parliament and the parliamentary law of Masonry, has never hitherto been written. The present work, as an initiative attempt to supply a long recognized deficiency, is fraternally offered to the Craft.

ALBERT G. MACKEY. M. D.

1440 M ST., WASHINGTON, D. C.
May 1, 1875.

PARLIAMENTARY LAW

APPLIED TO THE

GOVERNMENT OF MASONIC BODIES.

CHAPTER I.

PRELIMINARY.

PARLIAMENTARY Law, or the *Lex Par-liamentaria*, is that unwritten law originally collected out of records and precedents* for the government of the Parliament of Great Britain in the transaction of its business, and subsequently adopted, with necessary modifications, by the Congress of the United States.

It must not be supposed, from the name, that no such law was known before the establishment of the British Parliament. It is evident that at all times when, and in all countries where, deliberative bodies have existed, it must have been found necessary to establish some regula-

---

* Such is the definition of Sir Edward Coke.

tions by which business might be facilitated.
The parliamentary law of England and America
has been reduced by long experience to the
accuracy of a science, but it is well known that
other, though simpler, systems prevailed in former times. In the Roman Senate, for instance,
although, judging from the character of such
productions as Cicero's Orations against Cati-
line, and his Philippics against Antony, rules of
order could not have been rigidly enforced; yet
we know from historic evidence that the proceedings of that body were regulated by an
established system of rules. The parliamentary
law of Rome was not so extensive as that of
England or America, but it was just as positive,
for all the purposes which it was intended to
accomplish. Thus, the times and places of meeting and adjournment of the Senate, the qualifications of its members, the number that constituted a quorum, and the mode and manner of
taking the question or of proposing and perfect-
ing a law, were all absolutely defined by statutory
regulations; the intention of which was, to secure
a faithful and orderly transaction of public business. A similar system prevailed in all the other
countries of antiquity, where deliberative bodies
existed. In the popular assemblies of the

Greeks, in their Senate of Five Hundred, their Court of Areopagus, and in all their legal or political meetings, the business was conducted by established rules of order.

But what was found requisite for the regulation of public bodies, that order might be secured and the rights of all be respected, has been found equally necessary in private societies. Indeed, no association of men could meet together for the discussion of any subject, with the slightest probability of ever coming to a conclusion, unless its debates were regulated by certain and acknowledged rules.

The rules thus adopted for its government are called its parliamentary law, and they are selected from the parliamentary law of the national assembly, because that code has been instituted by the wisdom of past ages, and modified and perfected by the experience of subsequent ones, so that it is now universally acknowledged that there is no better system of government for deliberative societies than the code which has so long been in operation under the name of Parliamentary Law.

Hatsell, in his well known work on " Precedents of the Proceedings of the House of Commons," cites the remark of Mr. Speaker Onslow that "the forms instituted by our ancestors operated as a check and control on the actions of the majority, and were in many instances a shelter and protection to the minority against the attempts of power." And Hatsell himself, whose long experience as Clerk of the Commons gives his opinion a peculiar weight of authority, says, that "it is not so material that the rule should be established on the foundation of sound reason and argument, as it is that order, decency, and regularity should prevail in a numerous assembly."

Of course, as private societies are restrained within inferior limits, exercise less extensive powers, and differ in their organization and in the objects of their association, many portions of the parliamentary law, which are necessary in the business of Parliament or Congress, must be inapplicable to them. But, so far as their peculiar character requires, the parliamentary law has been adopted for the government of these societies.

Seeing, then, how necessary it is that every association, convened for deliberative purposes, should have specific rules for its government, and seeing also that just such a code of rules, the result of the sagacity of wise men, and well tried by the experience of several centuries, is to be found in the parliamentary law, it is surprising that any one should be found who would object to the application of this law to the government of Masonic bodies; and yet there are Masons who really believe that the government of a Lodge or Chapter by parliamentary law would be an infringement on the ancient landmarks, and a violation of the spirit of the Institution. And these men, too, at the very time of their objecting, are benefiting by the lights and following the directions of this very law, to which they appear to be so inimical; for no presiding officer can recognize a speaker, put a question, or decide the results of a division without referring for the manner in which these duties are performed to the usages of parliamentary law.

There are, it is true, on the other hand, some Masons, not well instructed in the jurisprudence of the Order, and not conversant with those peculiarities of the organization, in which it differs from other associations, who would apply to it indiscriminately the rules of parliamentary law, and thus would decide many questions contrary to the spirit of the Institution. Both of these are wrong. There is a *mezzo termine*, or neu-

tral ground, on which it is wisest to rest.   Here,
as elsewhere, a middle course will be found the
safest: *Medio tutissimus ibis* — we shall consult
truth and propriety by avoiding all extremes.

The true state of the case is this: Masonry
has an organization peculiar to itself.   Wherever
this organization comes in conflict with that of
other associations, the parliamentary law will be
inapplicable.   Where, on the contrary, this organization does not differ in a Lodge from that
of other deliberative bodies, the rules of order
by which such a Lodge should be governed will
be best found in the provisions of the parliamentary law.   Let us illustrate this by examples.

Under the operation of the unwritten law of
Masonry a Lodge cannot adjourn, but must be
closed by the Worshipful Master at his good will
and pleasure.   Now, in the parliamentary law
there are provisions for the government of ad-
journments, such, for instance, as that a motion
to that effect is always in order, and must take
precedence of every other motion.   This rule is
applicable to all societies wherein the members
have reserved to themselves the right of adjournment; but is wholly inadmissible in a Masonic
Lodge, where no such right exists.   If, then, a
motion for adjournment should be made in a

Lodge, it would not be necessary that the presiding officer should refer for his instruction to the provisions of parliamentary law in reference to adjournment. He should at once declare the proceeding out of order, and properly refuse to entertain the motion.

Again, although the members of a Lodge cannot select the time of adjournment, they have an undoubted right to close at any time a debate, in which the Lodge may be engaged, when they deem it improper or inexpedient to continue the discussion. Now, there are various modes of closing a debate, all of which are defined and regulated by parliamentary law. One of these is by a call for the previous question. Although there is no positive law on the subject, yet the spirit of comity and courtesy which prevails in the Institution, the authority of the best Masonic jurists, and the general usage of the Fraternity, have concurred in the decision, that the previous question cannot be moved in a Masonic Lodge. All the provisions, therefore, of the parliamentary law, which refer to the subject of the previous question, are inapplicable in Masonry, and need not be studied by the Master of a Lodge.

But the other methods of closing a debate are not in this category. These methods are, to postpone to a time certain, to postpone indefinitely, and to lay on the table. Each of these methods must be inaugurated by a motion to that effect, and these motions are regulated by parliamentary law, having each an order of priority and preference, and two of them being debatable as to the expediency of adoption, while the third admits of no discussion, but must be put to the assembly immediately after it is made.   In all of these cases, it is necessary that the presiding officer should be conversant with the parliamentary law in the premises, if he would avoid confusion and facilitate the despatch of business.

Not only, then, is a thorough knowledge of parliamentary law necessary for the presiding officer of a Masonic body, if he would discharge the duties of the chair with credit to himself and comfort to the members, but he must be possessed of the additional information as to what parts of that law are applicable to Masonry, and what parts are not; as to where and when he must refer to it for the decision of a question, and where and when he must lay it aside, and rely for his government upon the organic law and the ancient usages of the Institution.

Hence a treatise which shall accurately define the parliamentary law in its application to the government of Masonic bodies, showing precisely the points in which it must be pursued and those in which it must be abandoned — which shall indicate the alternating prominence of the parliamentary law and the organic law of Masonry, and which shall thus present the presiding officer with a chart, pointing out the intricate channels and hidden rocks and undercurrents which render every discussion in a deliberative body liable to confusion, which give rise to turbulence, which needlessly protract business, and make doubtful the success of truth — cannot be unacceptable or unprofitable as a contribution to the jurisprudence of the Order.

I purpose, then, in the present work, to undertake such a task. Defining, accurately, the prerogatives of the chair and the privileges of the members, and the difference between the *business* and the *work* of a Lodge, — terms of great significance, and which have an important bearing upon the relations of the parliamentary law with the law of Masonry, — I shall proceed to lay down the rules and regulations by which the Master of a Lodge may be enabled to conduct the business of the body over which he has been called to preside according to those well-settled principles of government by which alone confusion can be arrested and order preserved.

Although the term Master of a Lodge is used for the sake of brevity of expression, and to avoid a needless augmentation of words, it must be understood that the remarks made in reference to that officer are equally applicable to the presiding officer of higher bodies, such as Chapters, Councils, and Commanderies, unless the character of the remark itself, or a specific notice made at the time, should indicate that the principle laid down is to be restricted to symbolic Masonry.

But it must not be inferred that what is said of the government of subordinate Lodges or Chapters, Councils or Commanderies, is equally applicable to the Grand Bodies in those respective divisions of the Rite. A Grand Lodge, for instance, has a different organization from that of its subordinates. The prerogatives of a Grand Master are more extensive than those of a Master; and the privileges of the representatives who make up the governing body are necessarily superior to those which inure to the members of the subordinate bodies. Hence there is some discrimination to be observed in the application of the parliamentary law to the government of Grand Lodges, Grand Chapters, Grand Councils, and Grand Commanderies. These will therefore be, on appropriate occasions, specifically referred to, as well as made in distinct chapters the special subjects of investigation.

In the next chapter I shall enter, as a preliminary labor, into an inquiry as to what are the prerogatives of the Master of a Lodge, and as to what are the privileges of its members ; an inquiry which will necessarily include a discussion of that important and interesting question : What is the difference between the *work* and the *business* of a Lodge ?   This, indeed, will be found to be, as we go on, a key for the solution of many of the most difficult problems of Masonic parliamentary law.

CHAPTER II.

OF BUSINESS LODGES AND OF WORKING LODGES.

AMONG the differences which distinguish a Masonic Lodge from any other society, one of the most peculiar is, that the Lodge presents itself to us in the twofold aspect of an association for business and an association for work. The *business* of a Lodge is that which it does, in common with other societies; such, for instance, as the regulation of its financial affairs and the adoption of such measures as circumstances may from time to time require, for the good of the Lodge, or the convenience of its members. The *work* of a Lodge is the technical term intended to denote the reception of candidates and the conferring of degrees.*

The business of a Lodge is conducted under the parliamentary law, so far as it is not repugnant to the peculiar character of the Institution.

* *Work* is the older word, and was exclusively used in the primitive rituals. The word *labor*, now more commonly employed, is, however, exactly synonymous.

But the work of a Lodge is regulated simply by
the will of the Master.   To it the parliamentary
law can in no way apply, and this arises from the
distinctive design of the Masonic organization.

A Lodge is defined in the old Charges to be
"a place where Masons assemble and work."
While thus assembled and at work, a Lodge of
Masons has a peculiar reference to those ancient
building associations from whom the society has
derived its existence and organization, and even
its name.   The operative Masons were engaged
in the construction of material temples.   The
speculative Masons are occupied in the erection
of a spiritual temple.   From the operative art,
the speculative science has borrowed not only
its technical language, its implements, and its
materials, to all of which it has given a spiritual
signification; but it has adopted its working
regulations for its own symbolic purposes.   Thus
the Master of the Lodge is the *master of the work.*
He lays down his designs upon the trestle-board,
that the craft may pursue their labors.   He alone
is responsible for the fidelity of the work, and
must therefore be invested with the most ample
power to carry into effect the designs which he
has prepared.   From the workmen — the members of the Lodge — he has a right to expect

3

implicit obedience.   His decisions in relation to
work or labor are final, and without appeal, so
far as the Lodge itself is concerned.   He may
be censured, overruled, and even suspended or
removed, by the superior authority of a Grand
Master or a Grand Lodge ; but the Lodge itself
has no power of supervision over the decrees or
the actions of its Master when it is at work.   The
principle of autocracy prevails in all the old
Charges and Constitutions by which the society
was governed in its earlier days.   These documents constantly speak of the Master as the one
who was to control the work, while the craft
were merely to obey his commands.   This principle has, therefore, been carried into the modern
Masonic Lodges, where the symbolic work of
speculative Masonry is governed by the same
regulations as those that were in use among our
operative predecessors.

Hence, to a Lodge when at work, in the technical meaning of the expression, the parliamentary law, or any other rules of order, would be
wholly inapplicable.   The will of the Master is
the rule of the Lodge.   What are called the
"Old York Constitutions," say that every work-
man shall receive his wages meekly, and without
scruple ; which, symbolically interpreted, means

that the decisions of the Master shall be accepted without question.

But the case is different when the Lodge, having completed its work, proceeds to the transaction of ordinary business. Rules of order are now required to regulate the discussions which spring up, and the parliamentary law, as it affords the best system, may now be applied to the government of the Lodge.

But a Masonic Lodge, even when engaged in business only, differs very materially from any other society. The features of undivided responsibility which pertained to the Master, and of implicit obedience which was required from the craft in the operative system, continue to exert their influence upon the conduct of a Lodge, not only when at work, but also when engaged in business; and even here, therefore, the parliamentary law must be applied with some modification. This will appear in the subsequent chapters of this treatise. But it must always be borne in mind, that whenever we speak of the application of parliamentary law to a Masonic Lodge, we mean a Lodge engaged in business, and not a Lodge at work; and this distinction between a business Lodge and a working Lodge must never be forgotten.

CHAPTER III.

OF A QUORUM.

THE parliamentary law provides that a deliberative body shall not proceed to business until a quorum of its members is present.* What this quorum is has to be settled by a specific regulation of each organization. Thus, in the English House of Lords three constitute a quorum, and forty in the House of Commons. In both Houses of the American Congress, and in many of the State Legislatures, a majority of the members is required to make a quorum. But, no matter what is the number, it is settled by the general parliamentary law, that no business can be transacted unless the quorum, whatever it may be, is present. The only exception

* *Quorum* is derived from the Latin form of commissions of the peace, which are addressed to several persons *of whom* (" quorum ") a certain number are required to form a legal board. Substantively, it denotes the number of persons belonging to an assembly, corporation, or society which is required to transact business.

28

to this rule is, that after waiting a reasonable time, if no quorum can be obtained, the members present may organize for the purpose of an immediate adjournment to some other time.

With the exception of this provision, the parliamentary law of quorums is applicable to Freemasonry, and indeed is made so by special regulations. In the technical language of our ritual, a Lodge, to be capable of doing work or transacting business, must be "just, perfect, and regular." A "just Lodge" is one which has the Book of the Law unfolded, with the square and compasses lying thereon; a "perfect Lodge" is one that consists of the requisite number of brethren; and a "regular Lodge" is one that has a warrant of constitution authorizing it to meet. The second only of these provisions refers to a quorum, but each is equally necessary to the validity of the meeting. In other words, no Lodge of Freemasons can be opened unless there be a sufficient number of brethren present, having a Bible, square, and compasses, and a charter, or warrant of constitution. According to Oliver, an exception in the English Lodges may be made in the latter case; for he says, that "after the Lodge has been legally recognized by the authorities and registered in the Grand

3*

Lodge books, the absence of the warrant would not vitiate the proceedings ; * but a different doctrine prevails in this country, where it is held that the presence of the warrant of constitution is essential to the legality of the proceedings.

As to the composition of a "perfect Lodge," that is to say, as to the number of brethren necessary to make a quorum for the transaction of business, the old Constitutions and regulations are silent, and the authorities consequently differ. In reply to an inquiry directed to him in 1857, the editor of the *London Freemasons' Magazine* affirmed that *five* Masons are sufficient to open a Lodge, and carry on business other than initiation: for which latter purpose *seven* are necessary. This opinion appears to be the general English one, and is acquiesced in by Dr. Oliver; but there is no authority of law for it. And when, in the year 1818, the suggestion was made that some regulation was necessary relative to the number of brethren requisite to constitute a legal Lodge, with competent powers to perform the rite of initiation, and transact all other business, the Board of General Purposes of the Grand Lodge of England, to whom the suggestion had been referred, replied, with an over

* Masonic Jurisprudence, chap. vi., sect. i.

abundance of cautious timidity, "that it is a matter of so much delicacy and difficulty, that it is thought advisable not to depart from the silence on the subject which had been observed in all the Books of Constitutions."

At a first glance, the authorized ritual would appear to promise us a solution of the problem. There the answer to the question in each degree, "How many compose a Lodge?" ought to supply us with the rule by which we are to establish the quorum in that degree. For whatever number composes a Lodge, that is the number which apparently should authorize the Lodge to proceed to business. The ritual has thus established the number which constitutes a "perfect Lodge," and without which number a Lodge cannot be legally opened.

According to this rule, seven constitute a "perfect" Entered Apprentice's Lodge, five a Fellow-Craft's, and three a Master Mason's. Without this requisite number, no Lodge can be opened in either of these degrees. In a Chapter of Royal Arch Masons nine Companions constitute a quorum, and in a Commandery of Knights Templars nine Knights,* although, under certain

---

* This is, by recent decisions, confirmed by the Grand Encampment. The old ritualistic rule made eleven a constitutional quorum in a Commandery of Knights Templars.

well-known circumstances, three Knights are
competent to transact business.

But in the provision of the ritual we meet with
certain practical difficulties, so far as symbolic
Masonry is concerned.   Thus, although it has
been prescribed that three are sufficient to open
a Master's Lodge, it is evident, to every one acquainted with the ritual, that it would be utterly
impossible to confer the Master's degree with
that number.   And therefore in this country the
authority of the ritual in respect to a quorum has
not been generally recognized, except for the
mere act of opening.

Looking to the facts that the petition for a
dispensation or charter must be signed by at least
seven Master Masons; that a Lodge of Entered
Apprentices must consist of not less than seven;
and that originally all working or subordinate
Lodges were composed principally of Entered
Apprentices, and were, therefore, Apprentices'
Lodges, the Grand Lodges of America, which
have adopted any explicit rule on the subject,
have generally agreed to consider seven as the
proper number to constitute a quorum for business in a Master's Lodge.   Chase seems, I think,
to have adopted the proper view of the subject,
when he says that "the minimum number to

whom a dispensation or charter can be granted, may be considered as the minimum number to constitute a quorum for the transaction of business.   If seven be the number necessary to form a Lodge, then seven is the number necessary to continue a Lodge and to transact its business." *

In the absence of any landmark or specific ancient law, written or unwritten, on the subject, I am, therefore, inclined to think that seven should constitute the proper quorum for work or business in any of the symbolic degrees.   A Master would be correct in opening his Lodge with two assistants on the third degree, because the ritual declares that three Master Masons constitute a "perfect Lodge."   But he would hardly be justified in balloting for candidates, or in making appropriations from the funds of the Lodge, when so small a number of the members, whose interests would be affected by either of these acts, was present.   And as to work, although a candidate who had been elected at a previous communication might be present, the nature of the ceremonies would preclude the possibility of the Master conferring the degree with only two assistants.

It would be better, after the Lodge had been

* Masonic Digest, p. 79.
C

opened with only three members, that the
Master, finding no accession to the number by
new arrivals, should close it without proceeding
to business or work.

I have said that the provision of parliamentary
law which permits less than a quorum to organize
for the purpose of immediate adjournment is not
applicable to a Masonic Lodge. Adjournment
is a mode of concluding business which is unknown in Freemasonry. The Lodge is opened
and closed at the "will and pleasure" of the
Worshipful Master, and hence, as a motion for
adjournment would be out of order, no good
could be accomplished by the temporary organization of a less number than a quorum. In Parliament or in Congress, the appointed time of
meeting having expired, it is necessary that a
new time should be appointed for the next meeting; for which purpose those present, although
less than a quorum, are permitted by their adjournment to designate that time.

But no such necessity exists in Masonry, for
the Master of a Lodge has the power of calling
the Lodge together at any time.

The quorum in Grand Lodges depends upon
special enactment, and differs in the different
jurisdictions. The quorum in a Grand Lodge is

generally reckoned not by the number of persons present, but by the number of Lodges represented. A Grand Lodge might be opened in the third degree with the quorum prescribed for a Lodge of that degree. But I do not think that it could proceed to the transaction of business, unless the number of Lodges required by its constitution was present. The same rule prevails in respect to the quorum of a Grand Chapter or a Grand Commandery.

CHAPTER IV.

OF THE PRESIDING OFFICER.

IN the absence of the Master of a Lodge, the Senior Warden, or in that of both the Junior Warden, assumes the chair. And it is not unusual for a Warden, in such case, to invite a Past Master of the Lodge who may be present to take the gavel. But whoever, for the time being, presides over the Lodge, is invested, for that time, with all the prerogatives of an installed Master, so far as ruling the Lodge is concerned. The possession of the chair gives this authority, and hence the installation of the Master is called by our English brethren "passing the chair." The Germans press this idea, by calling their presiding officer the " Meister im Stuhl,"* or the Master in the chair; and Latin Masonic writers use the expression " Magister Cathedræ," which conveys the same idea. Whoever, therefore, is

---

* Frequently, but less correctly, " Meister vom Stuhl."

in the chair, controls the Lodge. Even the Grand Master, if present, can exercise no discipline until he has taken the chair and assumed the gavel.

The duties of a Master are far more important, and his prerogatives and privileges more extensive, than those of the presiding officer of any other society. The latter is directed and controlled by the provisions of the parliamentary law, but these are applicable to the Master of a Lodge only with many modifications.

Hence, the Master of a Lodge, faithfully to discharge these important duties, should be possessed of no ordinary qualifications. He should unite firmness of decision with moderation of rule, and should have that spirit of conciliation, and that amenity of manners, which would temper the excitement of passions, and prevent or calm unpleasant discussions, with, at the same time, that rectitude of judgment, which will enable him to promptly seize the point of controversy in a question under debate, so that the rules of order, necessary to direct a discussion to its termination, may suggest themselves almost intuitively to his mind.

Besides the duties of opening and closing the Lodge and directing the work, the Master, in the

4

hours of business, becomes the moderator or regulator of discussions and debates, puts the motions which are presented to vote, declares the result, and decides all points of order. Each of these must become the subject of separate inquiry in succeeding chapters, because in each the Master will be controlled to a certain extent by the provisions of parliamentary law.

CHAPTER V.

IN every society, when the presiding officer has made a decision on any question, which is unsatisfactory to one or more of the members, it is usual to take an appeal from that decision to the assembly, which may by a vote sustain or overrule it. This is called the right of appeal, and is in accordance with the principles of parliamentary law, and rules are to be found in every legislative assembly for the exercise of the right.

But in a Masonic Lodge or Chapter, from the peculiar character of the Masonic organization, an appeal from the presiding officer to the body over which he presides is not known. An appeal may be taken to the Grand Lodge or the Grand Chapter; but an appeal made from the decision of the Master to the Lodge would at once be ruled by that officer as out of order.

This doctrine has been in this country definitely settled by almost every Masonic authority. It is true that, about twenty years ago, the subject was freely discussed, and that the Grand Lodge of Ohio and the committee on foreign correspondence of Tennessee, sustained the principle, that an appeal would lie from the decision of the Master to the Lodge. But this opinion met with no support from the Masonic jurists of the time, who all have concurred in the principle, that appeals to the Lodge from the decision of the Master are not in accordance with Masonic law; and the decisions of Ohio and Tennessee were in subsequent years repudiated and reversed in those jurisdictions.

An attempt has been made by a few writers to discriminate between the work and the business of a Lodge. Thus, the committee of foreign correspondence of Tennessee, in 1853, while admitting that, so far as the mere Masonic work of a Lodge is concerned, there is some plausibility in the argument against an appeal, says: " But to contend that no appeal, on any decision whatever, whether business or otherwise, can be taken to the body of the Lodge, is an assumption of power altogether too great to repose in the hands of any one individual."

This attempt to discriminate between work and business would soon lead to confusion. In

many instances it would be difficult to say
whether a question of order properly pertained
to the work or business of the Lodge, and hence
it is safer not to draw this distinction, which has
accordingly been repudiated by the highest Masonic authorities.

This theory is founded on the nature of the
Masonic organization. In the early history of
the Order, when it presented an almost wholly
operative character, the masses of the Fraternity
consisted almost entirely of Fellow-Crafts; while
those only were Masters who presided over the
workmen. Whether degrees existed at that time
or not, is a question that is now being agitated
by Masonic writers. It is, however, undeniable
that these Masters and Fellows constituted gra-
dations of rank. The Master alone was made
responsible to the lord for the perfection of the
work, while the Fellows were responsible to the
Master. Hence, one of the points of the
earliest of the old Constitutions, known as
the Halliwell MS., gave to the Master the
absolute power to dismiss a Fellow, and
required the workmen to "receive their pay
full meekly such as it might be," that is,
without doubt, hesitation, or objection, which is
equivalent to investing the Master with auto-

4 *

cratic power.*   Whence follows the doctrine, that there can be no appeal from his decision.

At the revival in 1717, a new division of the Fraternity presents itself.   There is no question of the institution at that time of distinctive degrees. Fellow-Crafts were then permitted to act as Wardens, and a Master presided over the Craft, which Master, according to the Charges approved in 1722, was required to be chosen from among "the most expert of the Fellow-Craftsmen." By this promotion it seems that he received the Master's degree. But the mass of the Fraternity, who constituted the members of the subordinate Lodges, with the exception of the officers, were Entered Apprentices, and the only degree conferred in the Lodges was that of Apprentice ; for the thirteenth general regulation, adopted in 1721, declares that "Apprentices must be admitted Masters and Fellow-Crafts only in

* The spirit of implicit obedience to the awards of the Master pervades all the old Manuscript Constitutions. Thus, for example, the Cooke MS. says (1. 860), "yf eny discorde schall be bitwene hym and his felows, he schall abey hym mekely, and be stylle at the byddyng of his master or of the wardeyne of his master in his master's absens." And the same spirit of obedience to the Graceman's, the Alderman's, the Warden's, or the Master's authority pervades the Constitutions of the English non-masonic gilds of the Middle Ages. Compare the collection of them laboriously made by Toulmin Smith in his work on "English Gilds."

the Grand Lodge, unless by a dispensation."
Hence, on the principle of subordination in
degrees, which constitutes the very life of the
Masonic institution, the decision of a Master
Mason cannot be reversed by the action of a
Lodge of Entered Apprentices.   Thus arose, in
the beginning, the Masonic doctrine, that no appeal can be entertained by the Lodge from the
decision of the Master ; and although this distinction of degrees between the Master and the
members no longer exists, it being required by
the modern Constitutions of this country, at least,
that all the members of a Lodge shall be Master
Masons, yet for other not less cogent reasons
the doctrine and the custom are both retained: for
the Master alone is still responsible for the good
conduct of his Lodge.   To him the Grand Master
and the Grand Lodge look for the preservation
of order and the observance of the laws and landmarks of the Institution.   It would, therefore, be
highly unjust to permit a Lodge to overrule the
decision of an officer burdened with so heavy a
responsibility.   If he commits an error, the appeal must be made to the Grand Lodge, which
alone has the power to reverse his decision ; for
in Masonic, as in municipal law, there is no wrong
without its remedy — *ubi jus ibi remedium.*

If, then, an appeal is made by any member to the Lodge from the decision of the Master on any question relating either to work or business, it is the duty of the Master to declare such an appeal out of order, and to refuse to entertain it. This is the well-settled law of Masonry on this subject.

Diffident Masters sometimes, doubtful of the correctness of their decisions, have permitted an appeal *by courtesy*. This, however, is clearly wrong ; for, as it has been well said, the admission of appeals by courtesy might ultimately become a precedent, through which the absolute right to take appeals would eventually be claimed.

In the case of a reasonable doubt, the Master may of course avail himself of the advice and counsel of the most experienced members of his Lodge, and especially of its Past Masters, before coming to a decision ; but, having arrived at that decision, and having officially announced it from the chair, it is irreversible by the Lodge.

On the question of appeals from the decision of a Grand Master or a Grand High Priest, in a Grand Lodge or Grand Chapter, the opinions of Masonic authorities are not uniformly on one side. The Grand Lodges of Alabama, Illinois,

and perhaps a few other States, permit an appeal
to the Grand Lodge from the decision of the
Grand Master. Bro. Abell, of California, who
stands high as a Masonic jurist, makes on this
subject the following remarks:

"We consider a Grand Lodge in these days
as simply the legislature of the Craft; and as it
is the supreme authority, beyond which there is
no tribunal, where an appeal can be maintained,
it seems a very absurdity that one man, the temporary officer of its own elevation, should be
permitted, unquestioned, to declare upon what
subject it shall or shall not deliberate, and with
despotic power to pronounce and maintain his
single opinion in opposition, as it may be, to the
united voice of the body which created him." In
this opinion Bro. Chase, the author of the "Masonic Digest," concurs.

The Committee of Foreign Correspondence
of the Grand Lodge of New York, adopted in 1852
a contrary mode of reasoning. They say: "We
think that no appeal lies from the decision of the
Grand Master, because he is, in his official position, required, like the Master in his Lodge, to see
that the Constitutions and laws of Masonry are
faithfully observed. He cannot do this if his
opinion or decision may be instantly set aside by

an appeal to that majority which is about to violate them.   In such case, also, he may close the
Lodge to prevent the violation; so that calm
reason teaches us that there is no other just rule
in the matter than that of the supremacy and inviolability of presiding officers."

Dr. Oliver is equally positive on this question.
He says:* "In some instances the Grand Master's ruling of itself will decide a controverted
question, and there is no appeal from his decision ;
and if he should ever abuse his power, there is no
existing law by which he can be called to account."

However cogent may be the reasoning of Bro.
Abell, (and I admit that the legislative character
of a Grand Lodge, as the supreme tribunal in its
jurisdiction, might seem to justify an appeal from
an improper decision of a Grand Master, as
affording the only remedy for a wrong,) yet I am
obliged to confess that all the precedents, and
with the few exceptions already quoted, all the
authorities, are in favor of giving autocratic power
to the Grand Master and, by analogy, to the
Grand Lodge; so that it may be considered as
the settled law of Masonry in this country, that
there is no appeal from the decision of the Grand
Master or Grand High Priest to the Grand Lodge
or Grand Chapter.

* Masonic Jurisprudence, chap. vii., sec. ii., p. 391.

In the year 1856, the General Grand Chapter of the United States adopted a resolution, " that an appeal does lie in all cases from the decision of the General Grand High Priest to the General Grand Chapter, which alone can, in the last resort, by vote of two-thirds of the members present, determine what is the Masonic law or custom." But at the same time it provided that this resolution, as a rule, should not be considered as operating or having any effect in the State Grand Chapters or subordinates.

In the same year the Grand Encampment of the United States adopted a similar resolution and a similar provision. The action of these two supreme bodies seems to have settled the point of law, that an appeal does not lie from a Grand High Priest to a Grand Chapter, or from a Grand Commander to a Grand Commandery.

CHAPTER VI.

OF MOTIONS.

THE members of every deliberative assembly — and it is in this aspect that we are considering a Masonic Lodge — are of course called upon, from time to time, to declare their will or judgment. This can only be done upon the presentation of a substantive proposition, upon which they are to express their opinion. This proposition is technically called a motion. The discussion upon its merits is the debate, and the judgment is arrived at by a vote, in which each member expresses his individual opinion. The greater number of votes, whether for assent or dissent, is considered an expression of the will of the assembly; because in parliamentary law the will of the majority, in general, is taken for the will of the whole.

Motions as thus defined are of two kinds, principal and subsidiary. A principal motion is one that proposes to express some fact, opinion, or principle of the assembly, and which, on being adopted, expresses that fact, opinion, or principle, A subsidiary motion is one which is intended to change the character of the principal motion, as a motion to amend, or to strike out, or insert certain words; or to control its disposition, as a motion to postpone its consideration, to refer it to a committee, or to lay it upon the table.

There is another class of motions, which in parliamentary language are called "dilatory motions," because their sole object is to delay the progress of business. They consist usually of motions to adjourn, alternated with motions to adjourn to a certain day. On each of these motions the ayes and nays are called, and thus the time of the assembly is consumed to the exclusion of the main question. This system was originally adopted for the protection of the minority, who are thus enabled to prevent, for a time, and sometimes effectually, the passage by the majority of a distasteful measure. In Masonic bodies these dilatory motions have no existence, because the duration of the debate and the conduct of business is under the control of the presiding officer. In Masonry, the minority find their protection in the benign principles of the Order

5   D

and in the justice and impartiality of the Master
of the Lodge.

I shall devote this and the four succeeding
chapters to the consideration of a principal motion — that is to say, a substantive proposition —
which has been presented to the Lodge for the
decision of its members, tracing its progress from
its presentation, through the debate which may
ensue thereupon, to its final adoption or rejection. I shall not encumber the subject at this
time with any remarks on the subsidiary motions
which may arise. In other words, I will suppose
that a motion expressing some opinion has been
proposed, that it has been fairly discussed, without any attempt to amend, postpone, or otherwise evade its immediate disposition, and that
the discussion has been followed by a direct vote
upon its merits.

In treating this subject of motions, four things
are to be considered:

1. The motion itself; how it must be offered.

2. The debate; how it must be conducted.

3. The vote; how it must be taken.

4. The announcement of the decision; how it
must be made.

CHAPTER VII.

OF THE MOTION ITSELF, AND HOW IT MUST BE OFFERED.

WHEN any member desires to make a motion, he rises and addresses the chair. Having offered his motion, it must be seconded by some other member. For it is well settled by parliamentary law, that no motion which is not seconded can be entertained.* The concurrence of two members is necessary to secure its consideration. Hence, if a motion is not seconded, it falls to the ground, and the chair and the Lodge will take no further notice of it. And this rule applies to all principal motions, but not, as will be seen hereafter, to all subsidiary ones.

The motion, being thus made and seconded,

---

* If a proposition is not seconded, the Speaker takes no notice of it, and nothing is done in consequence of it. —*Hatsell's Precedents*, ii. 120.

must be reduced to writing,* if insisted upon by any member; and it is a good rule, that every motion should be written out, as confusion or controversy as to its terms or language is thus prevented in the subsequent proceedings. Many Lodges have a provision to this effect in their by-laws; and where such provision exists the rule must, of course, be strictly enforced by the presiding officer. But, in the absence of such rule, the common law of Parliament gives any member the privilege of demanding that it be written. Hatsell, one of the best authorities on parliamentary law, says: "It is to be put into writing, if the House or Speaker require it, and must be read to the House by the Speaker as often as any member desires it for his information." This is the rule of the British House of Commons, and the same rule exists in both Houses of the American Congress.

The rule of the Senate is: "When a motion shall be made and seconded, it shall be reduced to writing, if desired by the President or any member, delivered in at the table, and read by the Presi-

* Hatsell tells us that more than three hundred years ago, April, 1571, the rule was adopted "that from henceforth men making motions shall bring them in writing," and the custom, he says, "has been uniformly adopted ever since." — *Precedents*, ii. 112.

dent before the same shall be debated." That
of the House of Representatives is in the following words: "Every motion shall be reduced to
writing, if the Speaker or any member desire
it."

In parliamentary law, a motion thus made, seconded, and reduced to writing comes at once
into the possession of the House.   But in the
practice of Masonry another step is to be taken
before we can arrive at that condition.   The
autocratic power of the Master, or presiding
officer of a Lodge, makes him the only and final
arbiter of questions of order.   The Master may,
therefore, declare that the motion is not in order
— that is, not capable of being entertained —
and decide that it shall not be received; and
from this decision there can be no appeal to
the Lodge.   The motion must be passed over
without discussion; or, if the Master neglects or
omits to make such ruling, it is competent for
any member to make a similar objection, which
objection shall be duly considered by the Master
without any debate.

When a motion in a Masonic Lodge is thus
made, seconded, reduced to writing, and not
overruled on a point of order by the Master, the
Lodge is then placed in possession of it.   The

5*

Master reads it from the chair, and says, "Are
you ready for the question?" If no one desires
to discuss its merits, the vote is to be immediately taken in the form hereafter to be described. But if there is a difference of opinion
among the members, some being in favor of and
others opposed to it, a debate will ensue, which
constitutes the second stage of the proceedings.

CHAPTER VIII.

OF THE DEBATE, AND HOW IT MUST BE CONDUCTED.

DEBATES in a Masonic Lodge must be conducted according to the fraternal principles of the Institution. In the language of Dr. Oliver, "The strictest courtesy shall be observed during a debate, in a Mason's Lodge, on questions which elicit a difference of opinion ; and any gross violation of decorum and good order is sure to be met by an admonition from the chair." It must always be remembered, that the object of a Masonic discussion is to elicit truth, and not simply to secure victory. Hence, those means of suppressing due inquiry, which are so common in popular assemblies, are to be avoided; therefore it is that the motion for the *previous question*, so frequently resorted to by parliamentary strategists, as a means of stifling debate and silencing the voice of the minority, is never admitted in a Masonic Lodge. The discourtesy which such a motion exhibits on the part of the majority, and its evident object to prevent inquiry, make it entirely antagonistic to the benignant principles of the Masonic institution. I have never, in my own experience, known the motion for the "previous question" to be made in any Masonic body, and I suppose that the incompetency of such a motion has never been doubted. Bro. Benjamin B. French, who, from his long experience as Clerk of the United States House of Representatives, had become an expert in the science of parliamentary law, and who was equally skilful in Masonic practices, said that "Freemasonry knows no 'previous question,' and no Masonic body should ever tolerate it."*

Another method adopted in parliamentary bodies and public assemblies, by which the further discussion of a proposition is attempted to be stifled, is by a motion to adjourn the debate. It must, however, be observed, that the Master of a Lodge, as the autocratic arbiter of order, always possesses the power to suspend the further discussion of any subject when, in his opinion, such discussion would tend to impair the peace and harmony of the Lodge, or otherwise injuriously affect the interests of Masonry. Yet the exer-

* American Quarterly Review of Freemasonry, vol. i., p. 325.

cise of this prerogative is one which no Master, not of a very arbitrary disposition, would exercise without reluctance. He would, unless there were imperative reasons to the contrary, desire to leave the prolongation or the discontinuance of the debate to be determined by the wishes of the members.

Under such circumstances, I see no reason why a motion to adjourn the debate might not be made, although the Master could, in the proper exercise of his prerogative, decline to put the motion to a vote. Should he, however, accept the motion, it must be governed by the principles of parliamentary law as applied to questions of that kind. Of these the only ones that are applicable to Masonic practice are: 1. That no member who has already spoken on the question is permitted to make a motion for the adjournment of the debate. 2. That if such a motion has been negatived, it cannot be renewed until there has been some intermediate proceeding. In parliamentary bodies, it is usual to alternate motions for adjournment of the debate with motions for the adjournment of the house. In a Masonic Lodge there could be no such alternation, as a motion for the adjournment of the Lodge is inadmissible; yet as the members, who, at an early stage of the debate, might be unwilling to stop, would perhaps at a later period become wearied and desire to put an end to a tedious discussion, it would be better to so interpret the parliamentary rule, as that the motion for the adjournment of the debate having been negatived should not be renewed until some time had elapsed, and of the sufficiency of that interval the presiding officer would be the proper judge.   3. That when a debate has been adjourned to a particular time, on its resumption it assumes the precise place that it had occupied when it was adjourned, and, therefore, no member who had already spoken before the adjournment can afterwards speak to the main question.   4. That although a member had already spoken to the question under discussion, he may also speak on the question of adjournment of the debate, because that is really a new question.   5. That the usual form of the motion is "that the debate be now adjourned." 6. That when such a motion is made and seconded, and admitted by the chair, it must be put to the Lodge, unless withdrawn by general consent, before the debate can be resumed.   All discussion ceases until the result of the motion is determined.   If adopted, the debate ceases at once, and the Lodge proceeds to other business.   If negatived, the debate goes on as before.

When, in a debate, a brother desires to speak, he rises and addresses the chair. The presiding officer calls him by his name, and thus recognizes his right to the floor. While he is speaking he is not to be interrupted by any other member, except on a point of order. If called to order by any member, the speaker is immediately to take his seat until the point is stated, when the Master will make his decision without debate. The speaker will then rise and resume his discourse, if not ruled out by the Master. During the time that he is speaking, no motion is permissible. Every member is permitted to speak once on the subject under discussion; nor can he speak a second time, except by permission of the Master.

The rule restricting members to one speech is in accordance with the general principles of parliamentary law,* and is founded on the very natural doctrine, that a fair discussion implies the right of every one to express his sentiments. But as this can be done in a single speech, a second one is prohibited, lest the speakers should

* It is essential, says Hatsell, to the despatch of business, that the rule and order of the House, that no member should speak twice to the same question, should be strictly adhered to ; and it is the duty of the Speaker to maintain the observance of this rule without waiting for the interposition of the House.—*Precedents*, vol. ii., p. 105.

become tedious by needless repetition, the discussion be inordinately prolonged, and the time of the assembly be unnecessarily wasted.

Some Lodges, however, are more liberal on this point, and, by a special by-law, permit each member to speak twice on the same subject; and such a rule would, of course, override the parliamentary law; but where no such by-law exists, the parliamentary law would come into operation, and must be rigidly enforced.

To this law there are two exceptions, which must now be noted:

First. Any member in a parliamentary body— that is, a body governed strictly by parliamentary usage — is permitted to speak a second time, and even oftener, by the consent of the assembly; but as this second speaking is actually a breach of the rules of order, which rules of order are on that point and for that occasion suspended or overruled, to enable the member to speak a second time, and as the decision of all questions of order in a Masonic Lodge are vested not in the Lodge, but in the Master, the power of granting this consent is, in Masonry, transferred from the Lodge to the presiding officer. Hence, in the application of the parliamentary law on this subject to Masonic bodies, we must make this distinction. By the parliamentary law no person is permitted to speak more than once on the same subject, except with the consent of the assembly. In a Masonic Lodge no brother is permitted to speak more than once on the same subject, except with the consent of the presiding officer, unless the by-laws give him the privilege of a second speech.

Secondly. The right of speaking twice is always given to the mover of the resolution, who, if he desires it, may close the debate; after which it would be out of order for any other member to speak. Parliamentary jurists are in doubt whether this privilege exists as a matter of right, or simply by the courtesy of the assembly. But that it does exist, and that it is constantly exerted, and has always been unquestionably recognized, is, perhaps, sufficient to make it a matter of right by the law of precedent. This privilege is acceded to the mover, not only on a principle of justice to himself, but of expediency to the assembly. It is to be presumed that the mover of a resolution must know more of the subject-matter which it embraces, or at least that he is better acquainted with the reasons which he thinks should induce the adoption of the proposition, than any other member. He ought, there-

6

fore, to be permitted, for his own justification, as well as for the information of his fellow-members, to reply to any arguments which have been made by its adversaries in the course of the debate, or to correct what he may deem any misstatements of facts by the opponents of the measure. But to accomplish these objects, it is necessary that he should confine himself to the arguments which have been advanced, or to the statements which have been made. His reply must be what a reply actually means, namely, that which is said in answer to what has been said by another, and nothing more. He can enter into no new field of argument, nor introduce any new topics which have not been touched upon by the previous discussion. If he does, his speech ceases to be a refutation of the arguments of his opponents, and the new arguments introduced by him in his second speech give them in turn the right to a reply, provided that the speakers so replying have not before spoken to the question. Thus, Cushing says: "If a member, therefore, in his reply, goes beyond the proper limits and introduces new matter, other members are at liberty to speak to the question."

There is nothing in these principles of parliamentary law which is opposed to or inconsistent with the landmarks of Freemasonry, or the peculiar organization of the Institution ; and, hence, this parliamentary law is strictly applicable to the government of a debate in a Masonic Lodge. The rule thus obligatory on a Masonic Lodge may be enunciated in the language of the sixty-third rule of the American House of Representatives, which I adopt as the simplest in its terms, the necessary change being made from leave of the House to leave of the presiding officer :

" No member shall speak more than once to the same question, without leave of the chair, unless he be the mover, proposer, or introducer of the matter pending, in which case he shall be permitted to speak in reply, but not until every member choosing to speak shall have spoken."

But if a change is made in the nature of the question by the introduction of a subsidiary motion, then the right to speak again accrues to every member, notwithstanding he may have spoken on the principal motion. Thus, if an amendment is offered, then, as the amendment introduces a new issue, the freedom of debate requires that all the members who desire shall be permitted to discuss its merits. The amendment assumes for the time being the character of a new motion, and the debate on it must be governed by the same principles that are applicable to the original motion. But the inquiry into the nature of amendments will occupy our attention in a succeeding chapter.

CHAPTER IX.

OF THE VOTE, AND HOW IT MUST BE TAKEN.

ALL the members who desire to express their opinion on the subject-matter which is presented in the motion having spoken, and the mover of the resolution, if he wishes to avail himself of his privilege, having replied to the arguments which have been advanced against the measure, the next thing to be done is to obtain the voice of the Lodge on the question that is embraced by the motion, and a formal expression of its opinion, whether favorable or otherwise. This is technically called "Putting the question," and, like all parliamentary proceedings, is conducted with certain forms, from which it is not safe to depart. As a general rule in parliamentary bodies, the question is put in this form: "So many as are in favor of the motion will say *aye;*" and then, "So many as are of a contrary opinion will say *no.*" But in Masonry it is a well-established rule — although often neglected — to take the opinion of the Lodge, not by the vocal utterance of *aye* or *no*, but by a *show of hands*.   In the "General Regulations of the Free and Accepted Masons, revised, approved of, and ordered to be published by the Grand Lodge [of England], January 28, 1767," a part of Article XIII. is in the following words:

"The opinions or votes of the members are always to be signified by each holding up *one of his hands:* which uplifted hands the Grand Wardens are to count, unless the number of hands be so unequal as to render the counting useless.   Nor should any other kind of division be ever admitted on such occasions."*   This rule is still in force in the Grand Lodge of England, without other change than that of making it the duty of the "Grand Wardens or Grand Deacons" to count the votes.   This mode of putting the question involves the necessity of a change of phraseology on the part of the presiding officer.   The usual formula in this country is as follows: "So many as are in favor of the

---

* This was a very ancient mode of voting.   In the popular assemblies of the Greeks, the suffrages were always taken by holding up the hands.   Hence voting was called *cheirotonia*, or "hand-extending," and a voter was a *cheirotonetes*, or a "hand-extender."   A "show of hands" still means, in English, the expression of a vote.

motion will signify the same by raising the right hand;" and then, "So many as are of a contrary opinion will make the same sign." In some Lodges I have heard this phraseology: "So many as are in favor of the motion will signify the same by the usual sign of the Order." But as raising the right hand is not what is technically understood as a *sign of the Order*, the expression is evidently incorrect, and therefore the formula first given is to be preferred.

If the number of hands raised on each branch of the question is so unequal, that there is no difficulty in deciding which number is the greater, the Master next proceeds to announce the result; which, however, will be the subject of the succeeding chapter.

But if the presiding officer has any doubt as to which side has the preponderance of hands, he may for his own satisfaction require the vote to be again taken, or direct the Senior Deacon to count the votes; or if, after making his announcement, any member is dissatisfied, he may call for a *division*.

In popular assemblies the vote is first taken by "ayes" and "nays," and the decision of the chair is based on the preponderance of sound, whether of the affirmative or negative side. As this de-

pends on the accuracy of the ear, the decision
may sometimes be erroneous.   Hence a division
may be demanded, so as to make the result certain by exact counting.   In a Masonic body,
when the votes are counted by the Deacon, as
there can be then no inaccuracy in the count, it
would seem unnecessary to call for a division,
and such would be the fact, were it not that there
is another source of error.   In taking the question in the ordinary mode, many on both sides,
from indifference or some other cause, neglect
to vote.   But when a division is called, every one
present is required to vote, unless formally excused; and hence a division, even after the count
of the Deacon, is admissible, because only in that
way can the opinion of every member be obtained.

This division of the Lodge is not to be confounded with a division of the question, which is
hereafter to be considered.   In the House of
Commons a division is made by one party going
forth and the other remaining in the House;
whence it becomes important who are to go
forth and who are to remain, because the latter
gain all the indolent, the indifferent, and the in-
attentive; and the general rule has therefore
been adopted, that those shall remain in who

vote for the preservation of the existing order of things, and those go out who are in favor of a change. A similar manner of dividing the House in the American Congress having been found inconvenient, the present rule was adopted, by which those in the affirmative of the question first rise from their seats, and afterwards those in the negative. This mode has been generally adopted in Lodges, and the count of the standing members is made by the Senior Deacon. When, therefore, a division is called for, those in the affirmative are requested to stand, who are to be counted by the Senior Deacon, and then those in the negative stand, who are counted in the same manner. It is a general principle of parliamentary law, that all who are present shall vote on one side or the other, unless excused by the House. As this rule is founded on the just principle, that no man shall be permitted to evade his responsibility as a legislator, the rule seems equally applicable to Masonic bodies, where every Mason owes a certain responsibility to the Order of which he is a member.

In the usual mode of voting, either with or without a division, it is difficult to enforce the rule, because it is impossible to determine with certainty those who have declined to vote.* In parliamentary bodies, when the yeas and nays are called, it is easy to enforce the rule; but it is not customary, and I think not proper, to demand the yeas and nays in Lodges. In Grand Lodges, where the members are responsible to a constituency whom they represent, the vote by Lodges is often called for, which is equivalent to demanding the yeas and nays ; and I have no doubt that in such cases every member is bound to vote, unless excused by the Grand Lodge.

The rule must also be enforced in a subordinate Lodge on the ballot for a candidate for initiation, where every member is required to deposit his ballot. And this is founded on the great principle of unanimity, as it is set forth in Article VI. of the General Regulations of 1721, where it is said that "no man can be entered a brother of any particular Lodge, or admitted to be a member thereof, without the *unanimous consent of all the members of that Lodge then present* when the candidate is proposed, and their consent is formally asked by the Master."

It is a well settled principle that on the ballot

---

* Yet it is competent for any one to call the attention of the chair to the fact that a certain member has not voted. The brother must then vote or offer an acceptable excuse.

for a candidate every member present must vote, for unanimity cannot be predicated of a ballot where even one has declined to deposit his ball.

In parliamentary law, the presiding officer is required to vote only when the House is equally divided, or when his vote, if given to the minority, would make the division equal whereby the question would be lost.

In so exercising the privilege of a casting vote, it is usual for the Speaker or Chairman to express the reason of his judgment, which has usually been to so vote on any measure as to give to the House the opportunity of further discussion, and not to make the decision final, unless some important principle was involved. Such a rule of courtesy should also direct the Master of a Lodge, who, in giving the casting vote on a closely contested question, should always respect as much as possible the doubtful opinion of the Lodge.

In parliamentary practice there is no regulation which gives to the presiding officer his own individual vote as a member in addition to the casting vote. No such rule exists in the English Parliament nor in the American Congress, either in the House or in a committee. In the House of Commons, it was claimed in 1836 by the chair-

man of a committee, but the claim was dis-
allowed by the House.   But it was subsequently
ordered that in committees on private bills " all
questions shall be decided by a majority of votes,
including the voice of the chairman, and whenever
the voices are equal, the chairman shall have a
second or casting vote." *

This is an exception to the general parliamentary law, but in Masonry it is the permanent
rule.   In a Masonic Lodge the presiding officer
is entitled to a vote like any other member, and,
in addition to this, gives a casting vote when the
Lodge is equally divided.   The parliamentary
rule, therefore, that when the House is equally
divided the vote is lost, can never apply in
Masonry, since on an equal division of the Lodge
the casting vote of the presiding officer always
gives a preponderance to one side or the other,
as the case may be.

I am not aware of any specific law or ancient
landmark which gives this supplemental casting
vote to the Master when there is a tie, unless it
be No. XII. of the " Old Regulations," adopted
by the Grand Lodge of England in 1721, which
says : "All matters are to be determined in the

* Treatise on the Law, Privileges, Proceedings, and Usages of
Parliament, by Sir Thomas Erskine May, K. C. B., p. 387.

Grand Lodge by a majority of votes, each member having one vote, and the Grand Master having two votes." And this law is still in force. Dr. Oliver says of the English usage that in case of an equality of votes the decision centres in the Master, but he makes no reference to his additional vote besides the casting one.* The practice of giving the Master two votes in case of a tie, is, I think, almost universal in this country. †

There are some other regulations of parliamentary law in reference to voting which seem applicable to Masonic bodies, because they are founded on the principles of right and expediency, and do not contravene any of the landmarks or Constitutions of the Order.

Thus, in putting the question, the affirmative must be put first, and then the negative, and until both are put it is no full question.

It is therefore a principle of parliamentary law, that after the affirmative vote has been taken, and before the negative has been put, it is in order for any member to speak, if he has not spoken before. This rule is founded on the principle, that

* Masonic Jurisprudence, p. 223.

† I have heard of a few exceptions, but they are not sufficient to affect the predominance of the rule.

7

every debatable question may be discussed up to the moment of its being fully put. Although I have very seldom known any member of a Masonic Lodge to avail himself of this privilege, yet I see no reason why it should not be accorded if demanded. Again, no member, who was not present when the question was begun to be put, can be allowed to vote or take part in the proceedings; nor any division be called for after the presiding officer has announced the result, if any new matter has intervened. A division must only be called for immediately after the announcement of the vote, and before the introduction of new business.

Such are the rules which govern a Masonic body in putting the question upon any matter which has been sufficiently debated, and by which the opinion of the majority of the members has been obtained. The next stage of the proceedings is the announcement of that opinion, as thus obtained, by the presiding officer. The form in which this announcement is to be made will constitute the subject of the next chapter.

CHAPTER X.

THE question having been thus put and decided by a majority of votes — for, except
in special cases, where the concurrence of two-
thirds or three-fourths of the voters present is
required for the adoption of a proposition, the
voice of a bare majority always rules — the next
stage is the announcement of the result. This
is to be done by the presiding officer, and must
be effected after a certain form. It might seem
indifferent what form should be adopted, so long
as the assembly is put in possession of the
knowledge that a decision has been arrived at,
and what that decision is. But it is scarcely
necessary to dilate on the expediency of forms
in all matters of business, or to quote any authority for their excellence as checks upon irregularity or arbitrary authority. The form adopted
in all deliberative assemblies is very nearly the
same; and that which has been found expedient

75

in other societies may very well be pursued in Masonic Lodges.

The presiding officer, having himself counted the uplifted hands on either side, or, in case of doubt or of a division, having caused them to be counted by the Senior Deacon, and the count communicated to him by that officer, should then announce the result in the following words: "The ayes have it — the motion is adopted;" or "The nays have it — the motion is lost."

The announcement having been thus made, any member who is not satisfied with the correctness of the count may call for a division,* which can never be refused if made at this time. The Master then puts the vote a second time, requesting those on each side to stand alternately while they are counted. The Senior Deacon, having first counted the affirmative voters, reports the number, and then counting those in the negative reports them also; upon which the presiding officer makes the announcement in the formula already described, and from this announcement, upon a division, there is no appeal. The subject is then closed, and cannot be reopened at the same communication, for it is a principle of parliamentary law, that no question

* Hatsell on Precedents, ii., p. 140.

can be again offered which is substantially the same as one upon which the House has already expressed its judgment. "This is necessary," says May,* "in order to avoid contradictory decisions, to prevent surprise, and to afford proper opportunities for determining the several questions as they arise. If the same question could be proposed again and again, a session would have no end, or only one question could be determined, and which would be resolved first in the affirmative and then in the negative, according to the accidents to which all voting is liable."

If, therefore, a question which has been determined by the Lodge should be again proposed at the same communication, either in the same language or in language substantially the same, if it had been negatived, or in language of a directly contrary import, if it had been adopted, it would be the duty of the Master to rule it as out of order, and refuse to present it for consideration.

The subject may, however, in some cases and under some conditions, be re-opened by a motion for reconsideration, the rules for making which will be hereafter discussed.

In those instances where a concurrent vote of

* Treatise on Law, etc., of Parliament, chap. x., p. 283.

7 *

more than a bare majority is required for the adoption of a proposition; as, for example, in voting on an amendment to the Constitution, which requires a vote of two-thirds or three-fourths for its passage, the formula of announcement is different. Here, the votes having been counted by the Senior Deacon and the result communicated to the Master, the latter makes the announcement as follows: "Two-thirds (or three-fourths, as the case may be) of the members present having voted in the affirmative, the amendment is adopted;" or "Two-thirds of the members present not having voted in the affirmative, the amendment is lost;" and the same form will be followed, *mutatis mutandis*, in all cases where a vote of two-thirds or three-fourths is required for the passage of a proposition.

I have been particular in the description of these forms, not because they are in themselves important, but because experience has shown that they constitute the best mode of communicating to the assembly the result of the discussion and vote through which it has just passed; and, although to those familiar with parliamentary forms the instruction may seem trivial, there are many Masters of Lodges who, not having had that advantage, will not find the information unacceptable.

Having thus disposed of independent motions, and shown how they should be offered and how they should be discussed, how the question should be put and how the result should be announced, I shall next proceed to the consideration of subsidiary motions. These, therefore, will constitute the subject-matter of the next chapter.

CHAPTER XI.

OF SUBSIDIARY MOTIONS.

HAVING treated in former chapters of principal motions, or, as they are technically called, "main questions," we come next to the consideration of "subsidiary motions," by which term, in the language of Parliament, is meant those motions which are made use of to dispose of the principal motion, either temporarily or permanently, without coming to a direct vote on it.

But as it is a general principle of parliamentary law, that two independent propositions cannot be at the same time before the assembly, and as these subsidiary motions have the especial privilege of being presented at any time, notwithstanding the pendency of another proposition and during its consideration, they are also called "privileged questions."

According to parliamentary law, when a question is under debate, no motion can be received except:

1. To adjourn ;
2. To lie on the table ;
3. For the previous question ;
4. To postpone to a day certain ;
5. To commit ;
6. To amend ;
7. To postpone indefinitely ;

and these several motions have precedence in the order in which they are arranged. Such is the modern rule in the popular branch of the American Congress. It differs from the former rule, as well as from that prevailing in the Senate, where the motion to *amend* is the last in order, all the other subsidiary motions taking precedence of it. And notwithstanding the new rule adopted in 1822, by the House of Representatives, whereby a motion to *amend* must be put before one to *postpone indefinitely*, the old rule, which is also that of the Senate, still prevails in all popular assemblages, and a motion to *postpone indefinitely*, while a motion to *amend* is before the meeting, is admissible, and, if adopted, carries the amendment, as well as the original motion on which it hangs, away from the assembly.

But of these subsidiary motions or privileged questions, it has already been shown that the motion to *adjourn* and that for the *previous ques-*

F

tion are repugnant to the principles which regulate the Masonic institution, and cannot, therefore, be applied to the government of Masonic bodies.

The only subsidiary motions that can be entertained in a Masonic Lodge, during the discussion of the main question, are the following:

1. To lie on the table;
2. To postpone indefinitely;
3. To postpone to a day certain;
4. To commit;
5. To amend;

which several motions have precedence in the order in which they are above arranged. That is to say, the main question being before the Lodge, a motion may be made to amend it. It may then be moved to commit the motion and the amendment to a committee for report. While this question is pending, a motion may be made to postpone the question to the next communication, or to any other specified time. This may be replaced by another motion, to postpone the further consideration of the motion indefinitely; and, lastly, before any one of these privileged questions has been put to the Lodge, a motion may be made to let the whole subject lie on the table; and this, if adopted, puts an end at once to all further discussion.

Or, a principal motion being before the Lodge, a motion to amend it may be offered, and immediately the whole four privileged questions may be presented at the same time by four different members. One may move to commit; another, to postpone to a day certain; a third, to postpone indefinitely; and a fourth, to lay the motion on the table. Then each of these questions must be put in the order of its precedence. The presiding officer will first put the motion to lie on the table; this being rejected, he will put that for indefinite postponement; if that is rejected, he will then put the motion for postponement to a day certain; on its rejection, he will put the motion to commit; that being lost, he will put the amendment; and, if that is rejected, he will conclude by proposing the main question or principal motion.

It will be seen that a motion to amend is the last in order, and that, when it is offered, there are four ways, besides and before rejection, by which it may be put out of the presence and possession, for the time being, of the Lodge. Yet as amendments are offered more frequently than any of the other secondary questions on the first presentation of the principal motion, and as the other subsidiary motions only affect the time or mode of consideration, while amendments are intended to change the form, the substance, and sometimes the very object of the main question, it seems proper that they should be first considered; after which the other subsidiary motions will be taken up in the order of their precedence: the one which overrides all the others being the first to be considered. We shall thus proceed by a descending gradation from the highest to the lowest, precisely in the order in which these various privileged questions would be put by the chair. The order of consideration will therefore be as follows:

1. Of amendments;
2. Of the motion to lie on the table;
3. Of the motion to postpone indefinitely;
4. Of the motion to postpone to a day certain;
5. Of the motion to commit.

Each of these will form the subject-matter of a distinct chapter.

CHAPTER XII.

OF AMENDMENTS.

ETYMOLOGICALLY, "to amend" is to make better, by expunging a fault. In the language of parliamentary law, to amend is to make a change, whether it be for the better or the worse.

When a motion is pending before a Lodge, it is competent for any member to propose an amendment thereto, which amendment having been seconded,* takes precedence of the original motion, that is to say, it must be considered and adopted or rejected, before the question can be put on the original motion. If the amendment be lost, then the question must be put on the original motion. If the amendment be adopted, the question will be on the original motion as so amended; and then, if this question be lost, the motion falls to the ground. The adoption of the amendment brings an entirely new motion, more or less altered from the origi-

---

* The amendment must, like the original motion, be seconded; but this rule is often neglected in popular assemblies.

nal one, before the Lodge, and the original motion disappears, and is no more heard of. The not unusual mistake of some presiding officers, in supposing that the adoption of an amendment precludes the necessity of putting the question on the original motion, must be carefully avoided. The adoption of an amendment is so far from adopting the motion which it amends, that it actually destroys it, and brings a new motion before the body. The change effected by the amendment has given a different form to the original proposition.

An amendment can only be made in one of these three ways, namely: by striking out certain words; by adding or inserting certain words; or, lastly, by striking out certain words, and inserting others.

1. *Striking out certain words.* A proposition may be amended by striking out a part of it, but the part so stricken out should not by its omission, affect the coherence or grammatical congruity of the remainder of the sentence from which it is to be omitted. The sentence left should present a correct grammatical construction. This is apparently a small matter, but the neglect of its observance frequently leads to awkward phraseology, which requires further amendments to correct it.

If an amendment to strike out certain words be rejected, no subsequent amendment can be offered to strike out the same words, or any part of them; but it may be again moved to strike out the same words or any part of them, with other words, provided the new proposition substantially differs in meaning and effect from the one previously rejected.   It is an essential rule that the new proposition shall differ substantially from the one previously rejected, because, as it may be stated once for all, it is a well-settled principle of parliamentary law, that no question can again be proposed during the same session (which, in reference to the business of a Lodge, is equivalent to the same communication) upon which the house has already expressed its judgment.   And this is a necessary rule " to avoid contrary decisions, to prevent surprise, and to afford a proper opportunity for determining questions as they severally arise."

In accordance with this principle, if the motion to strike out certain words prevails, no subsequent motion can be entertained to insert the same words or any part of them in the same place.   But a motion may be entertained to insert them or any part of them in another place, or to insert them or any part of them with other

words in the same place, provided that the addition of the new words constitutes a substantially
different proposition.

A motion may be made to strike out all after
the word "That," and such a motion would be in
order, as one of the legitimate means of defeat-
ing a proposition. If adopted, the effect would
be to reduce the original motion to a nonentity,
which in that case would be quietly passed over,
the Lodge proceeding to other business.*

The usage in the British Parliament, in putting
the question on striking out words, is not "Shall
the words be stricken out," but "Shall they stand
as part of the motion."   This custom is founded
on certain historical and political reasons, which
do not affect this country ; and hence, in American legislative assemblies, the question is a direct
one on striking out, which usage uniformly prevails.

2. *Inserting certain words.* The rules here
are the same as those applicable to striking out.
If an amendment to insert certain words be rejected, no motion can be entertained for the
insertion of the same words or any part of them

* May, in his Treatise on Parliamentary Law, (p. 276,) gives
two precedents of this kind which occurred in the House of
Commons.   The equivalent motion in the Congress of the United
States is to strike out the enacting clause of a bill.

in the same place, but it may be moved to insert
the same words in another place, or to insert
them or any part of them with other words in the
same place, provided the additional words make
a substantially different proposition.

On the other hand, if the motion to insert certain words prevails, no motion can afterwards be
entertained to strike them or any part of them
out. It is *res adjudicata;* the judgment of the
Lodge has been given, and it would be idle to
attempt to reverse it. But a motion would be
entertained to strike out these words or any part
of them with other words, provided, by the addition of those other words, a new proposition was
submitted.

3. *Striking out certain words and inserting
others.* This is a combination of the two preceding questions, and must be treated in the same
way. A rule of the House of Representatives
provides that a motion to strike out and insert
is not divisible, but must be put as a whole.
This is not, however, in accordance with the
general usage of popular assemblies, and would,
if enforced, be often productive of inconvenience.
Some members might be in favor of striking out
and inserting, others of striking out but not of
inserting, and others again might be opposed to

8*

any change.   The best method of giving to each of these an opportunity of expressing his opinion is by dividing the question.   Hence, on the demand of any member, the question may be divided, so as to make two — first on striking out, and then on inserting.*

The proper manner of stating the question is first to read the original passage as it stands; then the words proposed to be struck out; next those to be inserted; and lastly, the whole passage as it will stand when amended.   If desired, the question is then to be divided, and put first on striking out.†

During the pendency of the motion to strike out, it may be amended by motions to modify it so as to retain a part of the words.   The form of this proposition would be to leave out a part of the words of the amendment, which is equivalent to retaining them in the motion.

* Cushing is contradictory in the expression of his opinion on this subject.   He says (No. 1353) that "it is common in this country to provide that the motion to strike out and insert shall not be divisible," but he had previously stated (No. 1335) that the two motions must be "put consecutively to the question, first, to leave out the words objected to, and second, to insert the others proposed in their place."   This confusion of opinion seems to have arisen from his referring at one time to the rule of Congress, and at another to the usage of popular assemblies.   The latter has, 1 think, been properly considered in the text.

† Hatsell, ii., pp. 80–87.

If the motion to strike out prevails, then the next question will be on inserting the proposed words. Here, again, amendments may be proposed to change those words, by leaving out a part of them or by inserting new words. If the motion to insert prevails, then the words so ordered to be inserted will constitute a part of the main motion. If it is rejected, then the main motion remains with the words stricken out, and none substituted in their place.

But if the motion to strike out is rejected, then the motion to insert cannot be put. The resolve not to strike out is equivalent to one to retain, and if the words are to be retained, the other words cannot of course be substituted for them.

But because it has been resolved not to strike out certain words for the purpose of inserting others, it does not follow that a motion may not be made to strike out the same words for the purpose of inserting other and different words. The rule laid down by Jefferson* on this point is as follows:

A motion is made to amend by striking out certain words and inserting others in their place, which is negatived. Then it is moved to strike out the same words, and to insert others of a

---

* Manual, sect. xxxv.

tenor entirely different from those first proposed.
It is negatived.   Then it is moved to strike out
the same words and to insert nothing, which is
agreed to.   All this is admissible; because to
strike out and insert A is one proposition; to
strike out and insert B is a different proposition;
and to strike out and insert nothing is still different.   And the rejection of one proposition
does not preclude the offering a different one.

When the question is divided, and the motion
to strike out is first put and then that to insert,
Mr. Jefferson thinks that the same rule should
prevail, although he expresses the opinion
"doubtingly," because it may be thought that,
having decided separately not to strike out the
passage, the same question for striking out could
not be put over again.   It is, however, more
reasonable and convenient, as he admits, to consider the striking out and inserting as forming
one proposition, although put in two separate
questions.   Therefore it may be laid down that,
the motion to strike out having been rejected,
the motion to insert cannot be put, but that a
new motion may be made to strike out, for the
purpose of inserting other words, differing in
substance from those at first proposed; or a
motion may be made to strike out without any
motion to insert.

Any number of amendments may be proposed to a motion, and be all offered before the question is taken on any of them. But there is no other rule of precedence than that which comes from priority of presentation. They must be put in the order in which they were offered.

We are next to consider the nature of amendments to an amendment, and the rules which regulate them, and this will constitute the subject of the following chapter.

CHAPTER XIII.

OF THE MOTION TO AMEND AN AMENDMENT.

AS it is possible that the proposed amendment to an original proposition may be as objectionable to some of the members as the main proposition itself, and may seem, in their opinion, equally to require a change, and as the same condition might occur in reference to the amendment to the amendment, and so on *ad infinitum*, there would not seem to be any reason why the proposing of amendments to amendments might not be illimitable, or limited only by the will of the members of the assembly. But the fact is, that such a piling on of questions, to use the parliamentary phrase, would result in great confusion and embarrassment. "The line," says Jefferson, "must be drawn somewhere, and usage has drawn it after the amendment to the amendment, which is called the amendment in the second degree." This is a rule founded entirely on the principle of expediency; but the reason for it is so evident that all parliamentary bodies have concurred in recognizing its existence.

If any part of the amendment to the amendment be objectionable, the only way of effecting an improvement in it is to reject this amendment in the second degree; and then, after giving it the improved form which may be desired, to propose it again as an amendment to the amendment. Thus, pending a certain question, it is proposed to amend by inserting a form of words which may be represented by A B. This it is proposed to again amend by inserting C D after A B. This is admissible; but if it were desired to amend C D by adding E, so as to make it C D E, this would be an amendment in the third degree, and, therefore, would not be admissible. The only way of reaching this result would be to reject the proposition to insert C D after A B, and then to move an amendment to the amendment A B by adding C D E.

When an amendment to an amendment to an original motion is pending, the question must first be put on the amendment to the amendment. If this be adopted, or rejected, then the question will recur on the amendment; and if this be rejected, then on the original motion; or, if the amendment be adopted, on the motion as so

amended. All the rules which affect an amendment in the first degree are equally applicable
to one in the second, except that the latter cannot be amended.

Before dismissing the subject of amendments,
it may be proper to say that an amendment need
not be of the same character as, or germane to,
the original motion. Hatsell says that one way
of getting rid of a proposition is to make such
amendments to the question as to change the
nature of it, and to make it objectionable to those
even who proposed it. Thus, an amendment
might be offered to strike out everything after
the word "*Resolved*," and to insert new words of
an entirely different or even contradictory import.

CHAPTER XIV.

OF THE MOTION TO LIE ON THE TABLE.

JEFFERSON says, that "when the House has something else which claims its present attention, but would be willing to reserve in their power to take up a proposition whenever it shall suit them, they order it to lie on the table, and it may be called for at any time."

This was, undoubtedly, the original intention, under the parliamentary law, of the motion to lie on the table. With this view it was often made by the friends of a proposition, who, however desirous of entertaining it, were unable at that moment to consider it. But now this object is much better attained by a motion to postpone to a time certain. In modern American usage, the motion to lie on the table is made by the enemies of a proposition, and, as Barclay says, is intended to give it its "death-blow," for the measure so laid on the table is very rarely ever taken up again.

The motion to lie on the table takes precedency of all other motions, and when made the question must be immediately put without debate.

The motion to lie on the table is not debatable, because to permit debate on it would be to frustrate the very object for which the motion was made. It is moved to lay a proposition on the table, because it is supposed that the entertaining of that proposition would impede or postpone the consideration of other and more pressing business. Whatever may now be the intention of the motion, such was certainly, originally, its object. The motion to lie on the table is then made to prevent an interruption of the regular business. Now, to go into a prolonged discussion on the merits of this subsidiary question, would be only to prolong the delay and interruption, the very inconvenience sought to be avoided. Hence, the motion to lie on the table is to be put at once without debate.

When a motion to lie on the table has been rejected, it cannot be renewed unless some new matter shall have been introduced. Thus, if on the failure of the motion to lie on the table, a new amendment is offered to the original proposition, then the motion to lie on the table may be again made, but not until then.

The adoption of the motion to lie on the table

not only carries with it the immediate subject to which it had been directed, but also everything that, in parliamentary phrase, adheres to it: thus, a substantive proposition being before the assembly, an amendment has been offered to that proposition, and then an amendment is moved to that amendment. It is now moved that the amendment to the amendment lie on the table. If this motion is adopted, not only the amendment to the amendment, but the first amendment also, as well as the original proposition, go to the table.

The reason for this rule, if not immediately obvious, will be understood after a very brief consideration. Let us represent the original motion by the letter A; let the amendment be represented by B; and the amendment to the amendment by C. Now, when the amendment B is offered, the proposition before the assembly ceases to be A, and becomes by the proposed addition or incorporation of the amendment B, a new proposition, which may be represented by the form A B. Again: if to this amended form of A another amendment (C) is offered, then a new proposition, differing both from A and from A B, is presented for consideration and for action; and this new proposition, by the addition of C to A B, assumes the form which may be represented by A B C.

The only way to bring A B back to the assembly, from which it has been temporarily removed for the new formula which was made by the incorporation with it of C, is to reject, or, as the mathematicians would say, to eliminate C. The question must be categorically determined whether C shall be adopted or rejected. If it be rejected, then the formula to be considered would be A B, and if that be rejected then the discussion would be upon A.

But a motion that C shall lie on the table is not to reject or to eliminate it. It still remains an integral part of the last form or proposition which had been presented for consideration. You cannot consider A B, because that proposition was removed out of sight by the new formula A B C. If you refuse then to consider C, you cannot take up A B, for there is now no such proposition in actual existence. In the language of parliamentary law, C so adheres to A B as to make an integral part of it, and if it be laid on the table A and B must lie there too. In like manner and for a similar reason, if C should be rejected, and then a motion be made and adopted that B lie on the table, A must go to the table with it.

This rule, although very general, is not universal. In the business of legislative bodies there are a few exceptions to it. Of these only one, it appears to me, has any reference to the government of a Masonic Lodge : that is, that, on the reading of the minutes, a motion to lay a proposed amendment to the minutes on the table will not if adopted affect the minutes, which will remain as if no motion to amend had been made ; and, of course, a subsequent motion to confirm the minutes, without any reference to the amendment, may be entertained.

A motion to lay a motion for reconsideration on the table is attended with a peculiar effect, which will be noticed when we come to treat the subject of reconsideration of motions.

Lastly, it may be observed, that a motion to lie on the table may, like all other motions, if adopted, be reconsidered.

9*

CHAPTER XV.

OF THE MOTION TO POSTPONE INDEFINITELY.

THIS is peculiarly an American motion, unknown to the British Parliament, and first used in the Congress of the United States in the year 1806.

It is an adverse motion: that is, one to be used only by the opponents of a proposition; for it is equivalent, for all practical purposes, to a rejection. Its effect is to take the proposition to which it is applied out of the assembly for that session or meeting. The rule of the House of Representatives is, that "when a question is postponed indefinitely, the same shall not be acted upon again during the session."

A motion for indefinite postponement is debatable, but the debate is of a very limited character. The merits or demerits of the original proposition should form no part of the discussion, which should be rigidly restricted to the propriety or expediency of postponing the question. A skilful and experienced presiding officer will be careful to see that the debate does not transgress this narrow and prescribed limit.

CHAPTER XVI.

THE motion to postpone to a day certain is in general a friendly motion, that is, one which is made by the friends of a proposition to facilitate, or at least not to embarrass, its reception. When a proposition is presented to an assembly, for the consideration of which it is not then ready, perhaps from the pressure of more urgent business, or from the want of certain information not then in its possession, or from some other cause which makes the discussion of the proposition at that time inexpedient or inconvenient, a motion may be made to postpone its consideration to some certain day, or to make it the special order for that day.

The effect of the adoption of a motion to postpone to a day certain is to remove the proposition, with all that is connected with it, from the assembly until the day specified, when it comes up as a privileged question.

A motion to postpone to a day certain may be

amended by striking out the day and inserting another.

One form of postponing to a day certain, and in parliamentary bodies the most usual form, is to move that the question be made the special order for a certain day.   But the nature of this motion will be better treated when we come to the consideration of the subject of Special Orders.

The motion to postpone to a day certain is sometimes used by the opponents of a measure to stifle a proposition by naming some day when it will be impossible to consider the question ; as, in Congress, to a day beyond the end of the session, or, in a society, to a day which will fall after the adjournment of the body.   Such a motion is equivalent to a suppression or rejection of the proposition.

In Lodges and Chapters the motion to postpone to a day certain is seldom if ever used, but it is not unusual to employ it in Grand Lodges or Grand Chapters.   It is evident that such a motion would only apply to bodies which meet for several days.   In a Lodge or Chapter a motion is sometimes made and properly entertained to postpone the consideration until a later hour in the evening ; but the rules which govern such a motion are precisely the same as those which apply to the motion for postponement to a day certain, only that *hour* is substituted for *day*.

The debate on this motion, like that on the motion for indefinite postponement, is exceedingly limited, being confined to argument for and against the expediency of postponement, without any reference to the merits of the original proposition.

CHAPTER XVII.

OF THE MOTION TO COMMIT.

WHEN it is desired to make a fuller investigation of a subject than is likely to be obtained by a discussion in full assembly, it is usual to refer it to a committee, when it is said in parliamentary phrase to be committed, or if it has already been in the hands of a committee, it is then said to be recommitted. The usual form of the motion in a popular assembly is, that the subject be referred to a committee. If it be to a standing committee, the committee is named by the mover; and, if to a special committee, it is so stated, and the number of the committee is usually designated.

Sometimes it is provided by law that a subject shall, whenever presented, be referred to a committee, as in the case of a petition for initiation, or membership in a Masonic Lodge. In such a case, it is not necessary to make a motion for commitment or reference. The presiding officer will refer the petition, as a matter of course, under the general law, to the appropriate committee.

A motion to commit may be amended, as, for instance, by adding "with instructions to report."

The debate on a motion to commit, like that on a motion for postponement, is limited and in the same way; that is, it must be not on the merits of the original question, but on the propriety or expediency of committing it.

Sometimes the report of a committee is not satisfactory, and then a motion may be made to recommit it, with or without instructions, for the purpose of having an amended or altered report. The motion to recommit may be made at any time before the adoption of the report. If a motion to recommit is adopted, the whole matter is brought back to the condition in which it was at the time of the original appointment of the committee, and an amendatory or revisionary report is made at a subsequent time.

CHAPTER XVIII.

OF INCIDENTAL QUESTIONS.

INCIDENTAL questions are defined by Cushing to be "those which arise out of and are connected with (though they do not necessarily dispose of) other questions to which they relate, and which, for the time being, they supersede."

It is evident that there must be a vast number of questions which will be continually springing up during the discussion of any proposition, and which are suggested extemporaneously, by points in the discussion. These are called incidental questions, because they are really only incidents of the debate. It is impossible to anticipate all the questions that might thus arise in the course of a discussion. Five, however, being of more frequent occurrence and of a more important character than the others, may become the subjects of our consideration. These are:

1. Questions of order.
2. Questions for reading papers.
3. Questions on leave to withdraw motions.
4. Questions on suspending a rule.
5. Questions on taking the vote by yeas and nays.

Each of these will constitute the subject-matter of a separate chapter.

Before proceeding to the separate considera-tion of each of these incidental questions, it must be observed that they are always in order, and for a time take precedence of and suppress the question before the meeting, provided that they refer to that question. Thus it is always in or-der, during the discussion of any proposition, to move a question of order, or to read papers, or to withdraw a motion, or to suspend a rule, pro-vided that the point of order, the paper, the mo-tion, or the rule has a distinct reference to and a direct bearing on the proposition then before the assembly.

These incidental questions are also subject to the operation of subsidiary questions. Thus it may be moved to lay any one of them on the table, to postpone, or to commit it. As a gen-eral rule, however, the adoption of the subsidiary

10

motion does not necessarily carry the main proposition under debate with it; but, the incidental
question being laid on the table, or postponed,
or otherwise disposed of by a subsidiary motion,
the main discussion is resumed as if no such incidental question had been made.   This rule,
although general, is not universal, and the exception must be determined by the nature of each
question.

CHAPTER XIX.

OF QUESTIONS OF ORDER.

IN any assembly of persons met together for the purposes of deliberation and discussion, no satisfactory result can be attained unless the discussion is regulated by well-known and generally recognized rules. It is by such rules only that order and decorum can be maintained, discord and confusion prevented, and a concurrent harmony of opinion be reached. These are therefore the rules of order, and their importance is such that it becomes the interest of every member to see them enforced.

Rules of order relate to the present action of the body, not to any past or prospective proceedings. They prescribe the character of the motions that may be made, the time at which they ought to be made, and the precedency of one motion over another; they impose the necessary limits to debate, and indicate the bounds beyond which it is not lawful for a speaker to pass in his discussion of the question before the body.

Every permanent deliberative body adopts a code of rules of order to suit itself; but there are certain rules, derived from what may be called the common law of parliament, the wisdom of which having been proven by long experience they have been deemed of force at all times and places, and are, with a few necessary exceptions, as applicable to Lodges and Chapters as to other societies.

These universal rules of order, sanctioned by uninterrupted usage and approved by all authorities, may be enumerated under the following distinct heads, as applied to a Masonic body:

1. Two independent original propositions cannot be presented at the same time to the meeting. If a Lodge is discussing a motion, no other independent motion can be entertained, although a subsidiary one may, until the first motion is disposed of.

2. A subsidiary motion cannot be offered out of its rank of precedence. Thus, when a motion has been made to lay any proposition on the table, it would be a breach of order to attempt to supersede that motion by one to commit or to postpone. The motion to lie on the table must be first put. That being rejected, the other motion to commit or to postpone may be offered.

3. When a brother intends to speak, he is required to stand up in his place,* and to address himself always to the presiding officer. It is a breach of order to address any other member or brother during the debate.

4. When two or more brethren rise nearly at the same time, the presiding officer will indicate, by mentioning his name, the one who, in his opinion, is entitled to the floor.

5. A brother is not to be interrupted by any other member, except for the purpose of calling him to order, nor while he is on the floor can any motion be made or question put.

6. No brother can speak oftener than the rules permit, but this rule may be dispensed with by the Master, if he sees good reasons for doing so.

7. No one is to disturb the speaker by hissing, unnecessary coughing, loud whispering, or other unseemly noise, nor shall he pass between the speaker and the presiding officer.† All of these

* This custom of standing when speaking seems to have been derived from the usages of very early antiquity. "It is everywhere observable, in ancient authors," says Archbishop Potter, "that no person, of what rank or quality soever, presumed to speak sitting."—*Archol. Græca*, p. 86.

† We find this rule existing at an early period in Masonry as a specific regulation, independent of the parliamentary law.

are breaches of decorum, for which the offender may be called to order.

8. No personality, abusive remarks, or other improper language, should be used by any brother in debate. If used, the speaker should be immediately called to order by the presiding officer or any other member. In Parliament or in Congress, a member who has been guilty of disorderly conduct is summarily dealt with; and if he is disobedient to the repeated admonitions of the presiding officer, he has been even rejected from the House. There is, I think, no doubt that a similar power is vested in the Master of a Lodge, who may direct a disorderly brother to be excluded from the meeting if he persists in his misbehavior.

9. If the presiding officer rises to speak while a brother is on the floor, that brother should immediately sit down, that the presiding officer may be heard.

10. Every one who speaks should speak to the question. This is perhaps the most important of all the rules of order, because it is the one

---

Thus, in the Charges of 1722, the Mason is directed "not to interrupt the Master, or Wardens, or any brother speaking to the Master." And this regulation was derived from an older law extant in the MS. Constitutions of the fourteenth and fifteenth centuries.

most necessary for bringing the debate to a satisfactory conclusion. To speak impertinently, therefore — that is, to speak to points not pertinent and relevant to the subject under discussion — is always viewed as a gross violation of the rules of order. But commensurate with its importance is the difficulty of determining when it is violated. It is entirely within the discretion of the Master of the Lodge to decide how far a member should be indulged in a line of argument not precisely within the scope of the question under discussion. The principle has been laid down by an experienced authority, Mr. Speaker Cornwall, of the English House of Commons, that "no matter introduced into a debate, which the question before the House cannot decide upon, is regularly debatable;" and this may be considered as a correct expression of the rule. No subject should be introduced into a debate, the merits of which could not be decided by the question under discussion, and by that alone. "When a member is in possession of the House," says Sir T. E. May, "he has obtained a right to speak generally; but is only entitled to be heard upon the question then under discussion, or upon a question or amendment intended to be proposed by himself, or upon a point of order.

Whenever he wanders from it he is liable to be interrupted by cries of 'Question'; and in the Commons, if the topics he has introduced are clearly irrelevant, the Speaker acquaints him that he must speak to the question." *

11. As a sequence to this last rule, it follows that there can be no speaking unless there be a question before the Lodge. There must always be a motion of some kind to authorize a debate. "It is a rule," says Sir T. E. May, "that should always be strictly observed, that no member may speak, except when there is a question already before the House, or the member is about to conclude with a motion or amendment."¦†

Parliamentary courtesy, however, permits a member, who is about to make a motion, to speak in its favor before he actually proposes it, but always with the understanding that he will speak to the question, and that he will conclude by formally proposing his motion. It is, however, always better that the member should first make his motion and secure a second, before he speaks to it.

These rules of order are so essentially necessary to the decorous conduct of a discussion and

* Treatise on Parliamentary Law, p. 298.
† Ibid., p. 301.

to its successful conclusion in the resolution and
determination of the question which is its subject-matter, that every member is deeply inter-
ested in its observance.   The duty of maintaining
them belongs, it is true, in a peculiar manner, to
the presiding officer, who should ever be on the
alert to detect and check any breach of them.
But it is also the privilege as well as the duty of
every other member to exercise the same vigilance.   Hence, it is always in order for any member to rise to a point of order.

When a breach of order has occurred which
has escaped the notice of the chair, or even
before the chair may have had time to check it,
any member may call the attention of the presiding officer to the violation of the rule.   To do
so, he will rise from his seat and say, "I rise to
a point of order;" upon which the Master will
request him to state his point, the speaker objected to having taken his seat, where he remains
until the point of order is decided.   The point
being stated either orally, or, if required by the
chair, in writing, the Master gives his decision,
whether a violation of the specified rule of order
has been committed or not.   If the latter, he says,
"The point is not well taken," and directs the
speaker to resume his argument.   If the former,

he says, "The point is well taken," and either
prevents the speaker from further discussion, if
it is the discussion itself which is objected to as
being out of order, or directs the speaker to
resume his argument with the necessary caution,
if the objection has been to the manner or scope
of his speech.

In other societies, this decision of the presiding
officer, although generally acquiesced in, is sometimes objected to by one or more of the members, when an appeal is taken from the decision
to the meeting, who decide without debate
whether to sustain or to overrule the decision
of the officer. But as has already been shown,
there is in Masonry no appeal from the decision of the presiding officer on a point of order,
and that decision is therefore conclusive.

CHAPTER XX.

OF QUESTIONS FOR READING PAPERS.

NO member can be required to vote on any paper the contents of which are unknown to him. Hence, any member has a right to call for the reading of any paper — for instance, a report — which constitutes at the time the subject-matter of a proposition, if it has not yet been read.

But if the paper has already been once read, or if, although referring indirectly to the subject of discussion, it constitutes no actual part of the proceedings, then it can only be read by consent of the meeting, which consent must be obtained on a motion regularly made.

CHAPTER XXI.

OF QUESTIONS ON LEAVE TO WITHDRAW MOTIONS.

WHEN a motion has once been made and seconded, and read from the chair, it becomes the property of the assembly. If the mover, therefore, desires to withdraw it, he can only do so by consent of the meeting, which consent must also be unanimous. And there is reason in this; for if the meeting, notwithstanding the objection of any member, were to grant leave for the withdrawal of a motion, it could gain nothing by the proceeding, for the objecting member might immediately renew the motion.

It is not always deemed necessary to make a formal motion for the purpose of a withdrawal. The mover, who desires to withdraw his motion, asks permission to do so, the request being announced by the chair; if no one objects, the consent is supposed to be informally granted; but if any member says, "I object," the matter is dropped and the discussion continues.

The motion — or, in the form above stated, the

request — for permission to withdraw a motion
may be made at any stage of the proceedings
before the final vote is declared, and if adopted
or granted, it removes the proposition of which
it is the subject from the meeting at once, and
all further proceedings on it are suppressed or
cease.   But when an amendment has been proposed to a motion, the original motion cannot be
withdrawn until the amendment has first been
withdrawn or negatived,* and if the amendment
has been adopted, it is not in order for the mover
of the original motion to ask leave to withdraw
it.† By the adoption of the amendment, the
original proposition has changed its form and
ceased to be the same question, so that the proposer has no longer any control over it.

Questions for the withdrawal of papers are in
the nature of questions for the withdrawal of
motions, and are subject to the same regulations.
Reports of committees, petitions, or protests of
members, and all other documents of any kind,
when once presented to a Lodge — whether
they be read and received as information, or not
read and merely laid on the table, and their consideration postponed or referred to a committee

* May, Law of Parliament, p. 260.
† Wilson, Digest, p. 12, No. 79.

11

—become the property of the Lodge, and can
be withdrawn only upon motion or request, and
the consent of a majority of the members.   A
motion for the withdrawal of such papers is always in order.

But an exception to this ruling must be made
in the case of petitions for initiation, which by a
recognized law or usage of the Order cannot be
withdrawn after having once been presented to
a Lodge; and a motion for the withdrawal of
such a petition would always be out of order.
Although we can find no regulation to this effect
in any of the ancient Constitutions, yet the con-
stant and universal usage of the Craft has given
to it the force of an unwritten law, and the reason for its existence must be sought in the symbolic character of our Institution and its original
connection with an operative art.   The candidate
for Masonry has always been considered, symbolically, as material brought up for the building
of the Temple.   This material must be rejected
or accepted.   It cannot be carried elsewhere for
further inspection.   The Lodge to which it is first
brought must decide upon its fitness.   To withdraw the petition would be to prevent the Lodge
from making that decision, and therefore no petition for initiation, having been once read, can

be withdrawn ; it must go through the necessary form : hence a motion to withdraw it would be clearly out of order.

A different regulation prevails in Commanderies of Knights Templars. Grand Master B. B. French made, while presiding over the Order in this country, a decision in the following words :

"Commanderies, having exclusive power to decide all questions concerning membership, must decide all questions concerning petitions therefor by vote — such as whether or not a petition may be withdrawn, etc."

This decision was approved and confirmed by the Grand Encampment, at its session in 1862, at Columbus.

It is surprising that one so experienced as Grand Master French in parliamentary usage should have clothed the language of his decision in such ambiguous and inaccurate phraseology. From its terms we can gather only, and that merely by implication, that in a Commandery a petition for membership (which we may suppose to include a petition for initiation) may be withdrawn by a vote of the body. But we are left in doubt whether that vote shall be a vote of the majority, of two-thirds, or the unanimous vote of all present. We must therefore apply the ordinary rules of interpretation of documents and the principles of analogy, to enable us to determine what sort of vote is required to authorize the withdrawal of a petition which has been presented to a Commandery.

Now, we cannot say that the word "vote" means in this decision a *majority vote*, or *a two-thirds vote*, because, as the context declares that "all questions concerning petitions" for membership are to be decided by vote, this would include questions on admission as well as withdrawal, and thus it would follow that a ballot for admission need not be unanimous, which would be contrary to the recognized statutes of the Order, as well as the settled law of Masonry in its other branches.

In this uncertainty we must come to the conclusion, that the decision settles only one point — namely, that a Commandery may entertain a question as to the withdrawal of a petition for membership, which by a very liberal construction we may extend to petitions for initiation. But as the decision is entirely silent as to what number of votes is necessary to decide that question, we must settle that point by a reference to the character of the question, and to the manner in which questions of a similar character are settled.

Now, it is a rule in all Commanderies that every petition for initiation, when presented, must be referred to a committee, and on the report of that committee be subjected to a ballot. While this rule is in force, no petition can be withdrawn. A motion to withdraw it is equivalent to a motion to suspend the rule. It will be seen hereafter that no Masonic Lodge can suspend any of its rules or laws except by superior authority. But the decision of Grand Master French and its approval by the Grand Encampment gave to Commanderies the power of suspending the rule, which requires a ballot on a petition, and under the suspension of withdrawing it. But as no rule can be suspended except by general consent, unless otherwise provided by another rule, it follows that a withdrawal of a petition, which, as I have said, is to be considered in the character of a suspension of a rule, can only be done by general consent — that is, by a unanimous vote. And this is in better accord with the dignity of the subject; for if a Commandery were permitted by a mere majority vote to evade the responsibility of deciding on the character and qualifications of its candidates and to throw it on

11*

some other Commandery, to which, by this withdrawal, the candidate would be permitted to apply, much evil might, it is evident, arise, and much injury be inflicted on the Order.

I do not for a moment doubt that the withdrawal of petitions for initiation is contrary to the spirit of the Masonic institution, and I regret that any decision was ever made, from the loose terms of which the implied power of withdrawal can be extorted. But as this decision has been made the law of Templarism, all that can now be done is to guard and restrict its exercise by the most rigid interpretation. I therefore conclude that a motion to withdraw a petition for membership in a Commandery may be entertained, but can be decided in the affirmative only by a *unanimous* vote.

CHAPTER XXII.

OF QUESTIONS ON SUSPENDING A RULE.

THERE is a recognized power in every deliberative body to suspend any one of its rules for the purpose of considering propositions or transacting business which would be, under the general rule, out of order and not admissible.

It is a general principle of parliamentary law, that anything may be done by general consent, and therefore any rule may be suspended at any time by a unanimous vote. But under certain circumstances, provided by the rules themselves, a rule may be suspended by a simple vote of the majority.*

Hence, if the constitution of a Grand Lodge, or the by-laws of a subordinate Lodge, include a system of rules of order in which there is a provision for their suspension by unanimous consent or by the vote of a majority of those present, it

---

* In the House of Representatives, a rule can be suspended only after one day's notice and by a two-thirds vote, except in one case, where a bare majority is sufficient ; but the general usage in societies is to require a unanimous vote.

will be in order to move such suspension, which motion is not debatable, nor subject to amendment, nor can it· be laid on the table nor postponed indefinitely, but must be brought to a direct vote; nor, having been lost, can it be renewed for the same purpose; nor, having been adopted, can it be reconsidered.

But it must be remembered that all this refers, so far as a Masonic body is concerned, only to such rules as contain a provision for their suspension. When there is no clause in the constitution or by-laws which prescribes that a particular rule may be suspended and directs the mode of suspension, a motion to suspend would be out of order and could not be entertained.

It refers also only to mere rules of order, for it is now universally admitted by Masonic jurists that a subordinate Lodge has no power to suspend its by-laws. But on this subject I have written so fully in my work on Masonic Jurisprudence, that I cannot do better than to repeat here what I have there said.

From the fact that the by-laws of a Lodge must be submitted to the Grand Lodge for its approval and confirmation arises the doctrine, that a subordinate Lodge cannot, even by unanimous consent, suspend a by-law. As there is no error more commonly committed than this by unthinking Masons, who suppose that in a Lodge, as in any other society, a by-law may be suspended by unanimous consent, it will not be amiss to consider the question with some degree of care and attention.

An ordinary society makes its own rules and regulations, independent of any other body, subject to no revision, and requiring no approbation outside of itself. Its own members are the sole and supreme judges of what it may or may not enact for its own government. Consequently, as the members themselves have enacted the rule, the members themselves may unanimously agree to suspend, to amend, or to abolish it.

But a Masonic Lodge presents a different organization. It is not self-created or independent. It derives its power, and indeed its very existence, from a higher body, called a Grand Lodge, which constitutes the supreme tribunal to adjudicate for it. A Masonic Lodge has no power to make by-laws, without the consent of the Grand Lodge in whose jurisdiction it is situated. The by-laws of a subordinate Lodge may be said only to be proposed by the Lodge, as they are not operative until they have been submitted to the Grand Lodge and approved by that body. Nor

I

can any subsequent alteration of any of them take place unless it . passes through the same ordeal of revision and approbation by the Grand Lodge.

Hence it is evident that the control of the by-laws, rules, and regulations of the Lodge is taken entirely out of its hands.   A certain law has been agreed to, we will say, by the members.   It is submitted to the Grand Lodge and approved. From that moment it becomes a law for the government of that Lodge, and cannot be repealed without the consent of the Grand Lodge.   So far these statements will be admitted to be correct.   But if a Lodge cannot alter, annul, or repeal such law, without the consent of the Grand Lodge, it must necessarily follow that it cannot suspend it, which is, for all practical purposes, a repeal for a temporary period.

I will suppose, by way of example, that it is proposed to suspend the by-law which requires that at the annual election all the officers shall be elected by *ballot*, so as to enable the Lodge on a particular occasion to vote *viva voce*.   Now, this law must, of course, have been originally submitted to the Grand Lodge and approved by that body.   Such approbation made it the enactment of the Grand Lodge.   It had thus declared that in that particular Lodge all elections for officers should be determined by ballot. The regulation became imperative on the Lodge. If it determined, even by unanimous consent, to suspend the rule, and on a certain occasion to proceed to the election of a particular officer by acclamation or *viva voce*, then the Lodge was abrogating for the time a law that the Grand Lodge had declared was binding on it, and establishing in its place a new one, which had not received the approbation of the supreme tribunal. Such a rule would therefore, for want of this confirmation, be inoperative. It would, in fact, be no rule at all — or worse, it would be a rule enacted in opposition to the will of the Grand Lodge. This principle applies, of course, to every other by-law, whether trivial or important, local or general, in its character. The Lodge can touch no regulation after the decree of the Grand Lodge for its confirmation has been passed. The regulation has gone out of the control of the Lodge, and its only duty then is implicit obedience. Hence it follows that it is not competent for a subordinate Lodge, even by unanimous consent, to suspend any of its by-laws. Should such a proposition be made, it would be the duty of the presiding officer to rule it out of order, and to refuse to entertain the question.

CHAPTER XXIII.

OF QUESTIONS ON CALLING FOR THE YEAS AND NAYS.

IN all American legislative assemblies it is provided, that on any pending question a vote by yeas and nays may be called for; that is, that the vote of each member shall be openly given and recorded in the journal. The object of this proceeding is to secure the responsibility of the representative to his constituents, who are thus enabled to know how he voted, and to call him to an account, should he have voted contrary to the views or principles which he was elected to represent.

It is evident that there can be no necessity for such a proceeding in a Masonic Lodge, where every member is independent and responsible only to God and his own conscience for the votes which he may give. The call for the yeas and nays being, then, repugnant to the principles upon which the Masonic institution is founded, if a motion or call for that purpose were to be made, the Master of the Lodge should very properly rule it out of order.

But a different system prevails in conducting the business of Grand Lodges, which consist of representatives, responsible to a constituency whose instructions they are bound to obey. Hence, in these bodies, a vote by Lodges, which may be considered as equivalent to a vote by yeas and nays, is allowed and sometimes prescribed by positive rule.

The calling in Grand Lodges for the vote by Lodges must in all cases, where the constitution of the body has provided no special rule on the subject, be governed by the general parliamentary law which regulates the vote by yeas and nays.

Any member may demand the vote by Lodges; and if there is a provision in the rules of the Grand Lodge which requires a certain number to concur in the demand, it is the duty of the Grand Master or presiding officer to ascertain whether there is that requisite number. This would be most conveniently done by calling on those who were in favor of the vote by Lodges to rise, when the votes would be counted by the Senior Deacon.

The demand for a vote by Lodges may be

12

made at any time, not only during the voting on
the question in another form, but even after the
decision has been made by the chair, provided
the Grand Lodge has not proceeded to other
business.

If a demand for the vote by Lodges has been
once made and refused by the Grand Lodge, it
is not in order to make the demand a second
time on the same question. But the demand
or motion for a vote by Lodges having been
negatived, it is in order for any one who voted
in the majority — that is, on the negative side —
to move for a reconsideration of the vote, which
preliminary question will be settled by a mere
majority vote.

While the vote is being taken, and at any time
before the decision is announced by the chair, it
is permitted to any member to change his vote.

The parliamentary rule is, that no one shall
be permitted to vote on a call for the yeas and
nays who was not "within the bar;" that is, in
the house when the question was stated. But I
do not think that this rule has ever been rigidly
enforced in Grand Lodges, where every member
is permitted to vote on such an occasion, if
present during the roll-call, although he may
have been absent when the question was stated.

CHAPTER XXIV.

OF QUESTIONS OF PRIVILEGE.

IN all parliamentary or legislative bodies there occur certain questions which relate to matters affecting the dignity of the assembly or the rights and privileges of some of its members, and these are hence called "questions of privilege." Such, for instance, are motions arising out of or having relation to a quarrel between two of the members, an assault upon any member, charges affecting the integrity of the assembly or any of its members, or any other matters of a similar character. Questions referring to any of these matters take precedence of all other business, and hence are always in order.

It is impossible to make a complete enumeration of all these questions, and parliaments, congresses, and legislatures have generally been guided by the precedents supplied by the decisions of former sessions in deciding what are questions of privilege.

The analogies existing in many respects between a Masonic Lodge and a legislative assembly leave no doubt in my mind that in the former, as in the latter, questions of privilege may arise. The only difficulty to be encountered is as to what matters can occur in a Lodge or Chapter that would properly give rise to questions of privilege. But as any proposition that involves a question of privilege is to be considered in preference to any other business, it is important that the presiding officer, whose duty it is to decide the point of order, should have some guide by which he may arrive at a correct decision. The following list, although necessarily incomplete, is presented as an approximation to a catalogue of what may in a Masonic assembly be deemed questions of privilege :

1. Any matter which affects the character of a member. Hence questions relating to charges of misconduct are questions of privilege, and may be presented at any time; and it is a principle of parliamentary courtesy to grant an unusual latitude to the member who is making a personal explanation, because of its importance to his reputation.

2. Matters that affect the character of the Lodge, such as false and scandalous reports of its proceedings.

3. Matters affecting the secrecy or safety of the Lodge, where a brother deems it necessary to give the proper precautions.

Under these three heads, I think, may be embraced all those subjects usually enumerated in works on parliamentary law as questions of privilege so far as they refer to a Lodge.

A question of privilege is always in order. Whenever a member rises and says, "I rise to a question of privilege," the question must first be stated. The presiding officer will decide whether it is or is not such a question. If he decides that it is, then the consideration of any other business whatsoever that may at that time be before the Lodge must be suspended until the question of privilege is disposed of.

And this disposition of the question may be either by entertaining it at once, and deciding it on its merits, or by any other of the modes of disposition to which any other question is subject. It may be ordered to lie on the table, be postponed definitely or indefinitely, or be committed for investigation and report to a committee. In the last case the character of a question of privilege adheres to the report, the presentation of which will always be in order, and will take precedence of all other business. But it does not

12 *

follow that the immediate consideration of and
final action on the report must be had ; for the
report, like the question to which it refers, is subject to the operation of any of the subsidiary
motions, and may, like any other report, be laid
on the table, postponed, or recommitted.

Questions of privilege, it must be remembered,
are entitled to presentation at any time, for in
this consists their privilege ; but that privilege
does not extend to their consideration.   Having
been once presented, they become, as to the time
and manner of their consideration, subject to the
rules which affect all other questions.

When the question of privilege has been disposed of in such a manner as may be deemed
proper or expedient, the subject of discussion or
proposition which had been interrupted and suspended by its introduction, is at once resumed
at the precise point at which the interruption had
intervened.

CHAPTER XXV.

OF PRIVILEGED QUESTIONS.

THERE is another class of questions, called "privileged questions," which are not, however, to be confounded with the class considered in the previous chapter; for although all *questions of privilege* are *privileged questions*, it does not follow that all *privileged questions* are *questions of privilege*. Strictly speaking, in the language of parliamentary law, questions of privilege relate to the house or its members, and privileged questions relate to matters of business.

Privileged questions are defined to be those to which precedence is given over all other questions. They are of four kinds:

1. Those which relate to the rights and privileges of the assembly or any of its members;

2. Motions for adjournment;

3. Motions for reconsideration;

4. Special orders of the day.

The first of these classes has been discussed in the preceding chapter. The second, or motions for adjournment, it has been heretofore shown, are unknown in the usages or in the parliamentary law of Masonry, and may therefore be dismissed without further discussion. The third and fourth will constitute the subject-matter of succeeding chapters.

CHAPTER XXVI.

OF THE MOTION FOR RECONSIDERATION.

BY the original parliamentary law, a motion for reconsideration is not a privileged question. Indeed, in the English House of Commons, whence our laws of parliament have derived their origin, the question of reconsideration is unknown. There a question, having been once carried, cannot be questioned again, but must stand as the judgment of the House; and when a bill is once rejected, another of the same substance cannot be proposed at the same session. This rule has often led to much inconvenience, and many expedients have been resorted to for obviating its effect; such as to pass an act to explain, or to enforce and make more effectual, or to rectify the mistakes of an act which has been once, however unwisely, passed.

Nothing could possibly be more absurd than such a regulation, which forbids all change of opinion; and therefore the American House of

Representatives has adopted a rule, that a motion for reconsideration, on the same day or the day after, is always in order, and shall take precedence of all other motions, except motions to adjourn. Hence, in this country, the motion for reconsideration has become a privileged question.

It is, however, regulated by certain rules, which prescribe the time when, the person by whom, and the questions on which, it may be proposed.

1. The motion for reconsideration must be made, says the congressional rule, on the same day or the day after. The operation of this rule in a Grand Lodge or Grand Chapter must evidently be the same. In a Lodge where the session does not continue beyond a day, or rather an evening, it is evident that the motion for reconsideration, to be within this rule, must be made at the same communication at any time before the Lodge is closed. Whatever has been done at one communication cannot be reconsidered at a subsequent one, any more than an act passed by Congress at one session can be reconsidered at another. If it is deemed advisable at a future communication to do away with a resolution which had been adopted at a preceding one, the proper motion would be not to reconsider, but to rescind or repeal.

2. No one who had voted in the minority on any question can move a reconsideration. The right of doing so is restricted to those who had voted in the majority.* And the reason of this is obvious: If it were permitted that those who had been defeated might seek to renew the contest in another trial of strength, then the time of the assembly might be wasted by the repeated efforts of the few, who were discontented, to obtain a reconsideration and a new discussion of questions which had been already settled by the many to their own satisfaction.

3. The motion for reconsideration can only be made in reference to matters that remain within the control of the meeting. Thus, when an appropriation has been made, and under its authority the Treasurer has paid out the money, it will be too late to move a reconsideration of the resolution making the appropriation. Indeed, where the order consequent on a resolution has been only commenced and not yet executed in full,

---

* That is, on the winning side. There may be questions where the majority will be the losers. Thus, on a motion to amend the Constitution, where a two-thirds or three-fourths vote is required, a majority of the members may vote for the amendment and yet there may not be enough of them to make the required constitutional majority of two-thirds or three-fourths. Here the minority are evidently the winners, and a motion for reconsideration must be made by one of them. It is always the winning side that must make the motion.

strict parliamentary law deems it improper to
move a reconsideration, although the completion
of the order may be prevented by a resolution
to discharge or rescind so much of it as yet remains unexecuted.   But this would not be technically a reconsideration of the question.

There are several rules in relation to motions
for reconsideration which require notice:

1. A motion for reconsideration is not debatable, if the question proposed to be reconsidered is not.   Cushing lays down a different
rule, but in the House of Representatives, where
the practice of reconsideration first arose, it has
been frequently decided that debate cannot be
allowed on a motion to reconsider a question
that was not itself debatable.

2. Although an original proposition may require for its adoption a vote of two-thirds or three-
fourths, the motion for its reconsideration may be
carried by a mere majority.

3. When a motion for reconsideration is made
within the proper limit of time, and the consideration of it is postponed to a day beyond that
time, if then it is withdrawn by the mover, it cannot be renewed: the time for making such a motion has passed.   But here it must be remarked,
that if the session of the body, in which such
motion for reconsideration has been postponed,

should terminate without any action on such postponed motion, it would fail. Thus, in a Grand Lodge, if a motion to reconsider a question should be postponed to the third day of the session, and the Grand Lodge should close without acting on the motion for reconsideration, it would fall to the ground, and the original proposition would remain in force. This is founded on an opinion expressed by two Speakers of the House of Representatives, that "where the term of the members expires without acting on the motion to reconsider, for the want of time or inclination, the motion of course fails and leaves the original proposition operative." *

4. When a motion for reconsideration has been decided either in the affirmative or negative, or while it is still pending, no second motion for reconsideration of the same proposition can be made. But if, on reconsideration, the proposition has been altered in form by new amendments, a motion for reconsideration will then be in order. To permit the same proposition, after reconsideration, to be again reconsidered, would be an idle waste of time and an unprofitable renewal of altercation.

5. A motion for reconsideration may be post-

* Barclay, Digest, 164.

13   K

poned definitely or indefinitely, or laid upon the table. If postponed definitely, or to a day certain, it is subject to the provisions already mentioned in a preceding paragraph. If postponed indefinitely or laid upon the table, the effect is to kill it, and to leave the original proposition in force. Indeed, in the House of Representatives, when it is desired to put a measure out of all reach of danger, it is an expedient often resorted to for the friends of the measure to move a reconsideration, and immediately thereon to move to lay the motion for reconsideration on the table. The effect of this proceeding is, that no second motion for reconsideration can be made, and the first cannot be taken up out of its order, which it is not probable will be reached, and the original proposition is thus secured as an accomplished and unchangeable fact. This is recognized parliamentary practice, and I see no reason why it should not be pursued in the proceedings of Masonic bodies.

6. The first effect of a motion for reconsideration is, that during its pendency the operation of the original motion is suspended. Thus, a resolution having been adopted to execute a certain act, and a motion to reconsider that act having been made, the act cannot be executed until the motion for reconsideration has been disposed of.

7. The effect of the motion to reconsider, if
it is carried, is to place the original proposition
in precisely the position it occupied a moment
before its adoption.   We are not carried back to
the form of the original proposition when it was
first introduced, but to the form which it had
assumed at the time that the final vote on its
adoption was taken.   Thus, we will suppose that
a resolution had been proposed, which we will
call A; to this B has been offered as an amendment, so as to give it the form of A B; and to
this again another amendment, C, has been proposed, so as to make it assume the form of A B C.
Both amendments being carried, the vote is
taken on the proposition in its amended form
A B C, and, this being adopted, a motion for
reconsideration is made and carried.   Now, the
effect of this will be to present to the assembly
for discussion, not the original proposition A, but
the proposition in its amended form, A B C.
The motion for reconsideration applies not to all
the preliminary proceedings, but only to the final
vote.   So, in parliamentary practice, when a bill
has been read a third time and passed, a motion
for reconsideration, if it prevails, places the bill
in the position of having received its second
reading, and not the first or the second, but only

the third reading is brought by the reconsideration before the house to be again acted upon.

8. When the motion for reconsideration has been carried, the original proposition to be reconsidered comes up immediately for action. It may be discussed, (if it is a debatable question,) amended, postponed, laid on the table, or subjected to any other operation to which it was liable during its original passage. And the effect of a successful motion for reconsideration is such, that even if the original proposition were not then before the assembly, but having been adopted, other measures had been acted on, it comes up immediately for action. In Congress it would at once take the place to which it belongs in the general order of business, or would go over to the next day on which business of the same description would be in order. But in a Lodge, whose session seldom exceeds a few hours, no such nicety of arrangement can be observed, and the discussion of the proposition ordered to be reconsidered must immediately follow upon the vote for reconsideration.

All that has been said in this chapter refers to the reconsideration of motions or resolutions. The reconsideration of the ballot is an entirely different thing, and will form the subject of the succeeding chapter.

CHAPTER XXVII.

OF THE MOTION FOR RECONSIDERATION OF THE BALLOT.

THERE is no question within the range of Masonic parliamentary law that is of graver importance than that which forms the subject of the present chapter. The great danger to the Institution is not from a decline by reason of its unpopularity, but rather from the too rapid and incautious admission of members, and hence the sacred and indefeasible right of a secret and independent ballot should be tenaciously guarded as the best security against such a danger. When fears are expressed by the leading minds of the Fraternity that the portals of the temple are too widely thrown open, it becomes necessary that all who wish well to the Order should see that its ancient purity is preserved, by a rigid and unalterable determination that, so far as their influence can avail, the inviolability of the ballot-box shall be maintained.

In a Lodge where every member has a correct

notion of the right of his fellow-members to express their preference for, or their opposition to,
a candidate for initiation, and where there is a
disposition to work harmoniously with a few
rather than discordantly with many, when a ballot is ordered, each brother, having deposited his
vote, quietly and calmly waits to hear the decision
of the ballot-box announced by the presiding
officer. If it is "clear," all are pleased that a
profane has been found worthy to receive a portion of the illuminating rays of Masonry. But
if it is "foul," each one is satisfied with the result, and rejoices that, although knowing nothing
himself against the candidate, some other member has been present whom a more intimate
acquaintance with the character of the applicant
has induced to interpose his veto, and prevent
the purity of the Order from being sullied by the
admission of an unworthy candidate. And even
if that candidate be his friend, and he has himself a conviction of his worth, he will not hastily
impugn the motives of the one who has cast the
black ball, but will generously suppose that circumstances and proper influences, of which he
has no cognizance, have led to the rejection.
Here the matter ends, and the Lodge proceeds
to other business.

But this harmonious condition of things does not always exist. Sometimes an injudicious brother, over-zealous for the admission of the applicant, becomes dissatisfied with the result, and seeks by a defence of the candidate, and by impugning the motives of some of those who voted against him, to induce the brethren to desire a new trial, in the hope of a more successful verdict.

A motion for a reconsideration of the ballot is the means generally adopted for obtaining this object, and it is proper, therefore, that the legality and regularity of this motion should now be discussed.

I commence then with announcing the proposition, that a motion to reconsider an unfavorable ballot is unauthorized by the parliamentary law of Masonry; would be at all times out of order; and could not, therefore, be entertained by the presiding officer. The elements necessary to bring such a motion within the provisions of parliamentary law are wanting. A motion for the reconsideration of any proposition must, as has already been said, be made, and can only be made by one who has voted in the majority or on the prevailing side; because, if this privilege were extended to those who had voted in the minority, who had been defeated, and were therefore naturally discontented, the time of the assembly would be wasted, and the members would be annoyed by repeated agitations of the same proposition; so that it could never be known when a question was definitely determined.

Now, as the vote on the application of a candidate is by secret ballot, in which no member is permitted to divulge the nature of his vote, there is no record of the votes on either side, and it is therefore impossible to know, when the motion for reconsideration is made, whether the mover was one of the majority or of the minority, and whether he, therefore, is or is not entitled to make such a motion. Nor is there any prescribed mode of arriving at that information. The presiding officer cannot ask the question, nor, if he should so far forget his duty as to propose the interrogatory, could the mover answer it without violating the principle of secrecy, which so rigidly adheres to the ballot. The motion would, therefore, have to be ruled out for want of certainty.

But although no motion for reconsideration can be made, there are circumstances which would authorize the Master or presiding officer of his own motion, to order a second ballot,

which may be considered as practically the same
thing as a reconsideration. Thus, on the first
ballot there may be but one black ball. Now, a
single black ball may have been inadvertently
cast—the member voting it may have been
favorably disposed toward the candidate, and yet
from the hurry and confusion of voting, or from
the obscurity of light, or the infirmity of his eyes,
or from some other equally natural cause, he
may have deposited a black ball when he intended
to have deposited a white one. It is, therefore,
a matter of prudence and caution that, when only
one black ball appears, the presiding officer
should order a new ballot, in the presumption
that on this second ballot more care and vigilance
will be exercised, so that the reappearance of the
rejecting ball will show that it was designedly deposited in the box. And the foundation of this
rule in sound sense and justice is so well admitted,
that in almost all Masonic bodies the by-laws
provide for a second ballot in cases where one
black ball appears in the first. But, if there
should be no such by-law, it is competent for the
presiding officer to exercise his discretion in the
premises, and direct a second ballot if he thinks
it is expedient.

But although it is the prerogative of the

Master or presiding officer, under the circumstances described, to order a reconsideration, yet this prerogative is accompanied with certain restrictions, which it may be well to notice.

In the first place, the Master cannot order a reconsideration on any other night than that on which the original ballot was taken. After the Lodge is closed, the decision of the ballot is final, and there is no human authority that can reverse it. The reason of this rule is evident. If it were otherwise, an unworthy Master might on any subsequent evening avail himself of the absence of those who had voted black balls to order a reconsideration, and thus succeed in introducing an unfit and rejected candidate into the Lodge, contrary to the wishes of a portion of its members.

Neither can he order a reconsideration on the same night, if any of the brethren who voted have retired. All who expressed their opinion on the first ballot must be present to express it on the second. The reasons for this restriction are as evident as for the former, and are of the same character.

It may be asked whether the Grand Master cannot, by his dispensation, permit a reconsideration. I answer emphatically, No. The Grand

Master possesses no such prerogative.   There is no law in the whole jurisprudence of the Institution clearer than this: that neither the Grand Lodge nor the Grand Master can interfere with the decision of the ballot-box.   In the sixth of the thirty-nine "General Regulations" adopted in 1721, and which are now recognized as a part of the common law of Masonry, it is said, that in the election of candidates-" the members are to signify their consent or dissent in their own prudent way, either virtually or in form, but with unanimity;" and the regulation goes on to say: "Nor is this inherent privilege subject to a dispensation, because the members of a Lodge are the best judges of it; and if a fractious member should be imposed upon them, it might spoil their harmony or injure their freedom, or even break and disperse the Lodge, which ought to be avoided by all good and true brethren."

This settles the question.   A dispensation to reconsider a ballot would be an interference with the right of the members "to give their consent in their own prudent way;" it would be an infringement of "inherent privilege," and neither the Grand Lodge nor the Grand Master can issue a dispensation for such a purpose.   Every

Lodge must be left to manage its own elections of candidates in its own prudent way.

From what has been said, we may deduce the following four principles, as setting forth, in a summary way, the doctrine of Masonic parliamentary law in reference to motions for a reconsideration of the ballot:

1. It is never in order for a member to move for the reconsideration of a ballot on the petition of a candidate, nor for a presiding officer to entertain such a motion.

2. The Master or presiding officer alone can, for reasons satisfactory to himself, order such a reconsideration.

3. The presiding officer cannot order a reconsideration on any subsequent night, nor on the same night, after any member who was present and voted has departed.

4. The Grand Master cannot grant a dispensation for reconsideration, nor in any other way interfere with the ballot. The same restriction applies to the Grand Lodge.

CHAPTER XXVIII.

OF SPECIAL ORDERS.

THE most common class of privileged questions in parliamentary assemblies is that to which is technically given the name of " orders of the day." When the consideration of any matter is, by a resolution, postponed to a certain day, the matter so assigned is called, when the day for its consideration arrives, the special order for that day.

By this act the order of the day becomes a privileged question, and takes precedence of all others. The parliamentary regulations which refer to this question are numerous and intricate, but very few of them have an application to Masonic Lodges or Chapters.

For instance, in all parliamentary assemblies the business is distributed by certain rules, which cannot easily be set aside. Thus, public motions must be considered on one certain day of the week; private ones on another. A third day is directed to be devoted to the consideration of

14

petitions, a fourth one to appropriations, and so on; so that the class of business which is arranged for one day cannot be discussed on another, unless this rule is suspended. Now, to make any question a special order for the day, and to give it precedence on that day over all other questions —over, in fact, the very class of questions that has been appropriated to that particular day— would be to violate the rules of the house. And therefore it has been decided that, when any proposition is made an order for a subsequent day, it is to be considered that the rules for that occasion have been suspended. But a rule cannot be suspended by the vote of a mere majority. A vote of two-thirds is required for that purpose; and therefore, to make any question a special order, it is necessary that two-thirds of the members should vote in favor of the proposition, although, when the special order comes up, a bare majority may postpone its consideration.

No such rule has been established in Masonry. A majority vote only is necessary in a Lodge or Grand Lodge to make any hour or day the special time for the consideration of any proposition; or, in other words, to make it the special order for that hour or day.

The limited period appropriated to the communication of a Lodge makes it very unusual to
adopt the practice of special orders; although a
proposition introduced in the early part of the
evening might be, and sometimes is, made the
special order for a later hour. But the protracted
session of a Grand Lodge or Grand Chapter often
gives rise to special orders; and therefore the
parliamentary rules that govern them, so far as
they are applicable to Masonic bodies, must be
considered.

The proper form of making any proposition a
special order is as follows: On the presentation
of any proposition, whether it be a motion, a
petition, an election, or any other substantive
matter, which it is then proposed to discuss, any
member may rise and say, "I move that this
motion (or whatever else it may be) be made the
special order for 10 o'clock on Wednesday morning," or any other hour and day that he may
select. This motion, being seconded, is put by
the presiding officer, and, if adopted by a majority of votes, the proposition becomes the
special order for that hour and day.

Accordingly, when the day and hour set apart
for the consideration of the special order has
arrived, that special order takes precedence of

all other business. The presiding officer or any member may call it up, and to do so may interrupt any one, although the latter may at the time have possession of the floor, and be addressing the meeting. Whatever business is then before the Lodge must be suspended at once, that the special order may take its place, and be brought before the assembly.

But, although the special order will thus obtrude itself before the Lodge at the sacrifice of all other business, it does not follow that it necessarily will retain the attention of the members. Like every other proposition, it is subject to various subsidiary motions. It may be discharged, or be postponed to another time.

If a motion to discharge the special order prevails, then it ceases any longer to be a special order. It loses its speciality and its privilege, and subsides into the class of motions to which it properly belongs, and can be called up only in the regular order of business, at the time when a motion to call it up would be in order. The business which had been suspended is at once resumed and proceeded with.

But a motion may be made, and may prevail, to postpone the special order to a future day or hour. The effect of this motion is different from that which discharges the order. The special order here loses its speciality and privilege only temporarily, and on the arrival of the time to which it had been postponed it resumes its special privilege, and may be called up as at the original time; still, however, subject to the same motions for discharge or for further postponement.

A special order may also be disposed of in a third way. Although it is the right, it is not the duty of any member to call up the special order. Hence, if a proposition has been made the special order for any hour of any day, and that hour passes without any action being taken to proceed with it, the special order is dropped, and can only come up thereafter as unfinished business and as an unprivileged question. The time appointed to consider it as a special order having passed, it loses its character as a special order.

Let us illustrate this usage. It is a very common practice in Grand Lodges to set apart a certain day and hour for proceeding to the election of officers for the ensuing year. Now, we will suppose that on Monday a motion is made, and that that motion prevails, making the election of officers the special order for 12 o'clock on Wednesday morning. When the hour of 12 on

14 *   L

Wednesday arrives, the Grand Lodge may be engaged in some other business, notwithstanding which, any member may call up the special order. If this be concurred in, the Grand Lodge proceeds to the election. But a motion may be made that the special order be postponed until 12 o'clock on Thursday ; and if this motion prevails, that hour is set apart for the election, and at that hour the special order again comes up. A motion may, however, be made to discharge the special order, and, if that motion is adopted, no future time is appointed for the election, and a new motion must be made to provide for it. Again, on the arrival of the hour of 12 on Wednesday no one may feel disposed to interrupt the business then in hand, and consequently no notice would be taken of the special order, which, in that case, would be dissolved, and the election could only be held in consequence of some future motion.

If, however, the motion to make the special order had been to make it " for Wednesday," and not for " 12 o'clock on Wednesday,"—that is to say, for the whole day, and not for any particular hour of it,—then it would be in order to call it up at any time during the session of Wednesday.

When a special order has been taken up, it

may be proceeded with to the exclusion of all other business until it is concluded. If not finished at the time of calling off, which in another society would be the adjournment, it is to be resumed the next day as unfinished business, having, however, the preference over all other business, unless a motion be made to postpone or to discharge it.

It is not uncommon for several orders to be made for the same day, in which case the one first made takes precedence of the others; and if the whole day is consumed by it, then the other orders lose their speciality, for they cannot be considered special orders for the ensuing day.

In Congress it is usual to frame the resolution making a special order so that the proposition is made "the special order for the —— day of ——, and from day to day, until the same is disposed of." A resolution so framed would carry over a special order from one day, when it had been omitted, to the succeeding day. This is not the form generally adopted in conducting the business of Grand Lodges, but I see no reason why it should not be; and if a motion in that form be made and adopted, the effect of it in a Grand Lodge would be the same as in Congress, where, although the first day may be consumed in the consideration of a special order previously made, the second one does not lose its speciality, but on the succeeding day comes up and takes precedence of all other business.

These are all the rules of parliamentary law in reference to special orders which appear to be applicable to the government of Masonic bodies.

CHAPTER XXIX.

OF THE ORDER OF BUSINESS.

THAT there may be no confusion or unnecessary delay in the transaction of business, that everything may be considered at the
proper time, and that due precedence may be
given to the most important matters, or to those
which claim precedence from some special reason,
it is necessary, in all deliberative assemblies, that
there should be some well understood arrangement, either by regulation or by custom, for the
government of the order and sequence in which
the various propositions that are likely to be
brought before the meeting shall be considered.

A settled order of business, says Jefferson, is
necessary for the government of the presiding
officer, and to restrain individual members from
calling up favorite measures or matters under
their special patronage out of their just turn, and
it is also useful for directing the discretion of the
members when they are moved to take up a particular matter to the prejudice of others having

165

priority of right to their attention in the general order of business.

Hence, an arrangement of business under proper heads and by a predetermined rule will be convenient to the Master of a Lodge, because he is thus enabled to carry on the business of the Lodge without unnecessary delay and embarrassment, and will be necessary for the government of the members, because by it useless and troublesome contentions for the precedency of propositions will be avoided.

In every Masonic body, therefore, the by-laws should prescribe an "Order of Business," and in proportion as that order is rigorously observed will be the harmony and celerity with which the business of the Lodge will be despatched.

In Lodges whose by-laws have prescribed no settled order, the arrangement of business is left to the discretion of the presiding officer, who will not, however, depend entirely on his own judgment, since he must be governed to some extent by certain general rules, founded on the principles of parliamentary law, or on the suggestions of common sense. Thus the propriety of getting rid of the unfinished business before any new propositions are entertained will naturally suggest itself as a rule of expediency; for if new propositions were permitted to be entertained before old ones, which had been proposed at former communications, were disposed of by their adoption or rejection, or some equivalent disposition of them, the business would so accumulate as to lead to confusion and embarrassment. It is, therefore, a settled rule of parliamentary law, that the consideration of unfinished business should take the precedence of that which is new. Again, there are certain propositions which, whenever they may arise, must be entertained, to the suppression of other matters for the time, because they are questions of privilege. And, lastly, there are special orders, the time for the consideration of which must have been provided at the time when their speciality was determined. Governed by these general rules, where, as I have already observed, no special rules have been provided, and exercising a wise judgment in the distribution of matters not coming under these heads, the presiding officer will find no difficulty in conducting the business of the meeting with ease to himself and with satisfaction to the members ; but if, on the contrary, he shall permit propositions to be introduced at improper times, irrelevant questions to be presented, and a regular arrangement to be neglected, he will

soon find himself involved in a labyrinth of per-
plexities, extrication from which will be difficult,
if not impossible; and, as this judicious manage-
ment of business constitutes one of the most
important functions of a Master of a Lodge as a
presiding officer, so does its absence or neglect
most strikingly develop his incapacity and unfit-
ness for the position which he occupies.

Experience has shown that the following arrangement or order of business is the one most
calculated to facilitate the consideration and disposition of the subjects that are usually brought
before a Masonic body, and it is the one, therefore, that has been most generally adopted.
After the Lodge has been opened, the process
of which ceremony, as it is prescribed by the
ritual, needs no explanation here, the first business is to read the minutes of the preceding
communication, and this is to be followed immediately by the question on their confirmation.
This refers only, however, to stated communications, because as the law of Masonry prescribes
that the proceedings of a stated communication
cannot be altered or amended at a special communication, it is not necessary nor usual at the
latter to read the minutes of a stated one that
had preceded it. The minutes, therefore, except

for information, are not read at special communications. The minutes, then, having been read and confirmed, the mode of doing which will constitute the subject of another chapter, the next thing will be the consideration of unfinished business. This will be presented by the Secretary, through the Master, to the Lodge in regular order. The reports of committees appointed at the former meetings will now be taken up for reading and consideration. Of these, the reports on petitions for initiation or affiliation take precedence of all others. If these reports are favorable, the next business will be the balloting for the candidates. Other reports of standing or select committees will be next in order. Those of select committees as seeming to have a more important character should take precedence of those of standing committees. Motions made at a former meeting and postponed for consideration, or laid upon the table, may now be called up: if postponed without reference to any hour, they will be in order at any time after the reception of and action on the reports of committees. If they had been postponed to a particular hour, they then become special orders, and can be called up only when that hour arrives; but whether in the one or the other category, it is

15

not the duty of the presiding officer to call the attention of the Lodge to such motions,* and if they are not called up by the special motion of a member, they will pass over without notice. The unfinished business being thus disposed of, the Lodge is now prepared for the consideration of any new proposition which may be presented, and the precedency of these propositions will be regulated by the parliamentary law as already described in the present work.

The presiding officer having learned, either by direct inquiry or by observation, that no further business is likely to be transacted, will direct the Lodge to be prepared for initiation, if there be any candidates in waiting; for this is always done after the business of the Lodge is transacted. After which the Lodge is closed.

It was formerly the usage, but one which is now too much neglected, to read the rough minutes of the evening before closing the Lodge, and this was done, not for their approval, because no question of confirmation was taken at the time, but that the members present might suggest to the Secretary the correction of any errors that he

---

* It is not his duty, but he may, like any other member, exercise the right, and therefore, if he chooses, he may call attention to the special order.

might have inadvertently made.   This practice, though peculiar to Masonic bodies, is a good one, and should not be neglected.

The order of business thus detailed may, for convenience of reference, be placed in the following tabular form:

1. Opening the Lodge.
2. Reading and confirmation of the minutes.
3. Reports on petitions.
4. Balloting for candidates.
5. Reports of select committees.
6. Reports of standing committees.
7. Consideration of motions made at a former meeting, if called up by a member.
8. New business.
9. Initiations.
10. Reading of the minutes for information and correction.
11. Closing the Lodge.

CHAPTER XXX.

OF THE APPOINTMENT AND FUNCTIONS OF COMMITTEES.

FOR the purpose of expediting business, by dividing the numerous labors of a deliberative body among various classes of its members, or to obtain the investigation of a particular subject more conveniently, by the inquiries of a few, than could be secured by the whole body, it has always been usual to appoint a certain number of members to inquire into and to report to the main body on any particular proposition, and the members thus appointed are called a *committee*, because the subject has been committed or intrusted to them for inquiry.

Committees are divided into two kinds, in reference to the subjects committed to them, and to the duration of their functions, and these two kinds are *standing* and *select*.

Standing committees are those to whom all propositions relating to a particular subject, as

they arise from time to time, are submitted.
Thus, to a standing committee on finance
would be referred all matters relating to the
funds of the Lodge, as their investiture or expenditure, and to a standing committee on charity
would be submitted all applications for aid and
relief.

Standing committees are usually appointed
at the beginning of the Masonic year, and continue in office until its close.   The mode of their
appointment depends on the provisions of the
by-laws, which sometimes designate the members, and sometimes direct them to be elected
by the Lodge or appointed by the Master.
Thus, as to the first class, many Lodges have
provided, that the first five or the first three
officers shall constitute a standing committee
on finance, to whom all financial matters shall
be submitted.   And, in reference to the other
class, it is also sometimes provided, that three
or five members shall be appointed by the new
Master, or elected by the Lodge on the night of
the annual election, who shall act as a committee
on charity, to whom all petitions for relief and
assistance made to the Lodge during the coming
year shall be submitted.   There may be other
standing committees, as, for instance, on the
15*

library, or on the hall, who are appointed in one
of the ways already designated; but to constitute
them standing committees, in the strict, technical sense of the term, their appointment or
election should be made at the beginning of the
Masonic year, and their functions should continue
until its close; and this appointment or election
should not be made under the authority of a
resolution, but of a special by-law or clause in
the constitution of the Lodge, just as standing
committees are formed under the rules appointed
at the beginning of the Congress. Committees
established at any other time, by a mere resolution, although they may be appointed for an
indefinite period, and may be directed to have
cognizance not of a single proposition, but of all
propositions of a particular class that may, from
time to time, present themselves for consideration, can be viewed only as *quasi* standing committees, but are really select committees, and
are to be governed in the mode of their appointment by the rules that regulate the appointment
of such bodies.

Select committees are appointed under a
resolution of the Lodge for the investigation and
consideration of some proposition which, having
been presented, it is deemed more convenient

should thus be inquired into by a few members, who can more readily than a large number put the matter into proper shape for the action of the whole body. In the discussion of this subject we are first to look to the mode of their appointment, and then to the manner in which they are to discharge their functions, which, of course, includes the question of their duties and powers.

In the first place, as to the mode of their appointment: Here the parliamentary and the Masonic law differ very widely. Anciently, in the English House of Commons, it was the practice, when a committee was ordered, for the members of the House to call out names for the committee, and for the clerk to take down the names without any formal question, until the requisite number had been obtained. But this practice has been abandoned, and it is now the usage for the person who moves for the committee also to move the names of those who are to compose it, each one being proposed separately, and the vote is then taken on his acceptance; and although, as a matter of courtesy, the list proposed is generally accepted, it is competent for the House to reject any one or all of them, and, by an amendment to each motion, to place some other member on the list in the place of the one rejected.

In the American House of Representatives the rule is for the Speaker to appoint all committees, unless otherwise specially ordered by the House, in which case they are to be appointed by ballot. But the latter mode is now never resorted to, and the present practice is for the House to direct the Speaker to appoint all committees, standing and select.

By the universal usage of Masonry, the appointment of all select committees, that is to say, all committees created by special resolution, is, unless otherwise specially provided for, vested in the presiding officer; therefore, when a motion is adopted which creates a committee, and charges it with the consideration of a particular subject, it is not necessary, as it is in other deliberative bodies, for the Master or presiding officer to inquire "How shall the committee be appointed?" Unless the resolution creating the committee provides at the same time for the election of its members by the Lodge, the power of the appointment is in the presiding officer.

In the motion for the creation of a committee the number of members is often left blank, and, after the adoption of the resolution, it becomes necessary to fill up the blank with some specified number. This may be done, as the filling of any other blank, by several motions for different numbers, in which case the presiding officer will put the question on each number, beginning with the highest, until one of them is adopted. But more frequently the blank is filled up upon the mere suggestion of some member, which suggestion is informally adopted if there be no opposition.

As to the number of which a committee is to be composed, there is no other rule than the pleasure of the Lodge; but uniform custom has restricted committees to as few as can conveniently and judiciously discharge the duty, on the ground that a few may be more easily brought together than many, are a less unwieldy body to organize, and can more readily agree upon measures. An odd number is also selected in preference to an even one, because, as a majority of the committee make the report, an odd number always secures a majority on one side or the other of the question, if there be a difference of opinion; whereas in an even number there might be a tie, and the committee could come to no conclusion.

The committee is appointed by the Master's reading out the names of the members whom he has selected, which duty he may perform at once;

M

or he may require time for a judicious selection, when he announces that he will make the appointment at his leisure.

There is no positive rule to regulate the presiding officer in the choice of committee-men, but the courtesy of parliamentary law has always indicated that the person who makes the motion for the creation of a committee should be the first one placed on it, and not to so name him would be considered as an act of discourtesy.

In naming the other members of the committee, respect should be had to their peculiar views of the subject to be referred. It is a parliamentary practice not to appoint persons on a committee who are opposed to the proposition which is to be referred. It being the object of a committee to prepare the matter with which they have been charged, and to put it into a shape fit for the action of the body which they represent, it is evident that they should be so far its friends as to lead them to such a result. The enemies of a proposition would be more likely to stifle it than to give it a proper form for future discussion. In the forcible language of a parliamentary writer, "The child is not to be put to a nurse that cares not for it." But where the proposition with which a committee is charged consists of several parts, it is no objection to the appointment of a member that he is opposed to some of these parts, so long as he is favorable to the general proposition. His partial opposition might lead him in the committee to propose such alterations and amendments as would give the entire subject a more acceptable shape in the Lodge when it was reported by the committee, than it had in its original form.

By courtesy the first-named person is considered as the chairman of the committee, and he is recognized as such, at least so far as to call the committee to order at its first meeting. But every committee has the right to select its own chairman, and may, at its first meeting, displace the one named by the presiding officer and elect another in his stead. This has sometimes been done, but the more general usage is to accept the first-named member as the chairman.

In strict parliamentary law, to give legality to the acts of a committee, it has been considered necessary that every member should be present at its deliberations, unless at the time of its appointment, or by some general rule of the body which has appointed it, the number required to constitute a quorum shall have been expressed. But this rule no longer exists in this country, and it is generally recognized as good parliamentary law that a majority of the members of a committee will constitute a legal quorum to do business.

Unless the time and place for the meeting of a committee have been specifically expressed by the body appointing it, these matters are left to the discretion of the committee, which, without such instructions, may meet at such time and place as to the majority shall seem most expedient and convenient. But a quorum of the committee must meet formally to transact any business; the opinions of the members cannot be taken by the chairman separately, from which opinions he is to make up his report. Everything agreed upon must have been submitted in committee, and an opportunity given for free discussion.

Business is transacted in a committee with less formality than in the deliberative body from which it emanates. The members are permitted to speak as often as they please, and are not required to stand when addressing the Chair. But all the rules which govern motions and questions in deliberative bodies are equally applicable to committees.

A committee is restricted to the consideration

and investigation of the proposition with which it is charged. It cannot go beyond it, nor take up other matters irrelevant to and unconnected with it. Appointed with a definite object, it must confine itself to that object.

A committee may adjourn from time to time, until a majority of its members shall have come to an agreement on the matter which had been referred to it. This agreement it announces to the body which had appointed it in a document drawn up by the chairman, or some other member of the committee appointed for that purpose. This document is called its report, which will constitute the subject-matter of the following chapter.

16

CHAPTER XXXI.

OF THE REPORT OF A COMMITTEE.

WHEN a committee, to which a subject had been referred, has completed its investigation and come to an opinion, it directs its chairman or some other member to prepare an expression of its views, to be submitted to the assembly under whose direction it has been acting. The paper containing this expression of views is called its report, which may be framed in three different forms: It may contain only an expression of opinion on the subject which had been referred; or it may contain in addition to this, a definite resolution or series of resolutions, the adoption of which by the assembly is recommended; or, lastly, it may contain one or more resolutions, without any preliminary expression of opinion.

The report, when prepared, is read to the members of the committee, and, if it meets with their final sanction, the chairman or one of the members is directed to present it to the assembly.

The mode in which the report thus prepared
is to be presented to the assembly next requires
attention.   In the British Parliament the presentation of the report of a committee is accompanied with several forms, which have long since
been abandoned in the parliamentary bodies
of this country.   And while in our popular assemblies and in Masonic bodies the forms of
reception and consideration of a report are still
simpler than they are in the National Congress
or the State Legislatures, they still preserve
enough of the spirit of the parliamentary law to
insure expedition and regularity.

Standing up in his place in the Lodge, the
chairman, or other member appointed for that
purpose, announces to the presiding officer that
the committee to which such or such matters
had been referred is ready to report.

The question which now ought to be put to
the meeting by the presiding officer is: "Shall
the report be received?"   But here the fiction
of the parliamentary law, like the fiction of the
common law in many cases, supplies the place
of fact, and the question is supposed to be put
and carried by the silent acquiescence of the
members, and the chairman then reads the report.

But although it is taken for granted, when

there is no opposition, that the report has been received, it is competent for any member to move that it be not received. The effect of the adoption of such a motion would, I think, be to suppress the subject altogether, and to dismiss its further consideration, unless a motion was also made to recommit the report. Cushing says, that "it is not apparent what the precise effect of the decision would be—whether the committee would be discharged and the matter there stop, or whether the refusing to receive the report would be equivalent to a recommitment;" but he admits that if the report so rejected be the final report of the committee, which had adjourned without day, the committee would be *functus officio*,— discharged from farther duty,—unless revived.

It is, I think, most reasonable to suppose that, if the assembly refuses to receive the report of the committee, the matter necessarily drops, unless revived by a subsequent resolution to recommit the report. The committee, in making its report, has accomplished the duty confided to it, and nothing more remains or is competent for it to do. To refuse to accept the report unconditionally, is to give the quietus not only to it, but to the subject-matter on which it is based.

But on the announcement of the chairman that the committee is ready to report, if a motion be made to receive the report, or if no express opposition being made, it is tacitly received, then the next thing is for the chairman to read it. The parliamentary usage is for the chairman to read the report in his place, and then to hand it to the clerk, who reads it again. But in popular assemblies and in Masonic Lodges this formality is not adhered to. Sometimes the chairman reads the report and sometimes the Secretary reads it for him, and it is not read the second time unless the second reading is called for.

The reading of the report is its reception. It is, therefore, an error, although a very common one among persons unacquainted with parliamentary law, to move, after it has been read, that the report be received. This has already been done, and such a motion would now be unnecessary and out of time.

The report having been received and read, the committee is thereby discharged, in the case of a final report, from any further consideration of the subject, and is virtually dissolved. It is unnecessary, therefore, to make a motion for its discharge.

The next question, then, that comes up is the
16*

disposition to be made of the report.   And here it is usual for the friends of the report to move that it be adopted.   Now, the report may be made, as has already been said, in three forms: as a mere expression of opinion, as that expression accompanied by resolutions, or simply as a resolution or series of resolutions.

If the report be in the first of these forms, it does not seem necessary to move its adoption. For as the opinions of a deliberative body can be expressed only in the form of resolutions, the adoption of a mere opinion can have no binding effect.   It is best, therefore, to let such a report pass without any motion whatever, and then it would go on the records simply as the opinion of the members of the committee.   If this opinion is to become operative as a rule of action, that can be effected only by some resolution based upon its recommendations, which resolution may be made by any member of the Lodge or assembly.   This is the parliamentary method of proceeding, but it is not always observed in Lodges, where the motion to adopt a mere declaratory report is often made.   But if the motion is carried, its effect is precisely that above stated. Such a motion has no more legislative value than the piece of paper on which it is written.

But the report may be submitted in its second or third form, that is to say, the expression of opinion may be accompanied with resolutions, or the report may consist simply of a resolution, or series of resolutions, not preceded by any preliminary expression of opinion.

Here the motion for adoption would be strictly regular, and its effect would be tangible.   If the motion to adopt a report having resolutions annexed, or consisting only of resolutions, be carried, then the adoption of the report is also the adoption of the resolutions, which thus become the expression of the will of the assembly, and have the same legal effect as they would have if they were resolutions which had been independently proposed by some member irrespective of the committee.

But, if the motion to adopt is lost, then the matter is defunct.   The effect of a refusal to adopt a report is the same as a negative vote on a motion.   By the refusal, it ceases to be before the body, and goes into parliamentary death.

But on the reception of a report there is another method, besides adoption or non-adoption, by which it may be disposed of.   Instead of moving that it be adopted, a motion may be made that it be recommitted.   If this motion be carried, the committee, which had become *functus officio* by the reception of its report, is instantly revived. The report is handed to the chairman, and the committee in due time makes another report, which passes through the same stages, and is governed by the same rules as in the case of the first report.

This recommitment may be accompanied with instructions, but these instructions can refer only to some legislative act, such as the preparation of a resolution for future action. In parliamentary bodies reports are often recommitted, with instructions to a committee to prepare a bill. Analogous to this would be the instructions of a popular assembly to its committee to prepare a resolution. But, in the case of the parliamentary body, the preparation of the bill by the committee is intended to expedite the forms of legislation. Nothing of this kind could be accomplished by causing a committee to prepare a resolution, since the resolution could be more readily offered by a member, and acted on at once by the assembly. It is not, therefore, usual to recommit reports with such instructions, although such a course would be perfectly regular and parliamentary. Sometimes, however, reports have been recommitted, with instructions to change the opinions therein expressed. This

is altogether incorrect and unparliamentary.
The members of a committee cannot be required to change their views on any particular
subject, merely to gratify a majority who hold
different views; and to require them to express
on paper an opinion that they do not entertain,
would be an unjust assumption of power.

The better course is, when the report of the
committee is objectionable, to reject it at once
on the question of its adoption. New resolutions can then be offered to meet the views of
the majority, independently of the report, if it
contain resolutions. If it was only the expression of an opinion without resolutions, the mere
reception of it does not give the sanction of the
body to the views expressed in it; but, if it be
thought necessary, a declaratory resolution in
opposition to the report might be offered and
adopted.

Committees go out of existence only on the
reception of their final report. Preliminary reports, for the purpose of asking information or
instruction in reference to the subject-matter
which has been referred to it, may be made by a
committee at any time during its session, without affecting its continuance.

Sometimes the stated period arrives for a
committee to make its report, which, however,

it is not prepared to do, in consequence of not having completed the investigation of the matter referred to it. The usage, then, is for the committee simply to "report progress, and ask leave to sit again." This being granted, the committee resumes its sessions and makes its report at some subsequent time.

What has been hitherto said refers only to select committees. Standing committees are governed by different rules. Their reports are always in order, and the reception of the report of a standing committee does not affect the continuance of the committee.

Minority Report.—It sometimes happens that one or more members of a committee will dissent from the views of the majority, and that they will naturally desire to express their antagonistic opinions in a written paper. This paper is usually called a "minority report." But the term is an inaccurate one, since the decision of parliamentary law is, that the minority of a committee cannot make a report, a minority not being a committee. Such reports are not known in the British Parliament, but in Congress, by a courtesy of the House, they are on motion received with the report of the majority and are printed, postponed, or considered in the same manner. Their effect seems to be to serve as a basis for

amendments to be moved in the resolutions proposed by the majority.   It has been usual,
although not strictly parliamentary, in popular
assemblies, when there are two reports, to move
that the report of the minority be adopted.   Such
a motion is only admissible on the ground that it
is to be viewed as a motion for a substitute, by
way of amendment to the report of the majority.
If such a motion is adopted, its effect is the change
of the character of the majority report, and the
adoption of the report as so amended.   But at
this stage a motion might be made to lie on the
table, to commit, or to postpone.   In a word, the
report of a minority can only be treated as any
other amendment to that of the majority.

One more observation is necessary.   The report of the minority does not, I think, so adhere,
in parliamentary phrase, to that of the majority,
that a vote to lay the former on the table would
carry the former with it.   It is one of the exceptions to the general rule, that whatever adheres
to the subject of a motion goes to the table
with it.

The report of a committee on the character
of an applicant for initiation or affiliation is a
matter peculiarly Masonic, and requires a special
consideration.   It will therefore constitute the
subject of the next chapter.

CHAPTER XXXII.

OF THE REPORT OF A COMMITTEE ON CHARACTER.

WHEN a petition for the initiation of a candidate into the mysteries of Masonry or for the application of a brother who has demitted from the Lodge to which he was formerly attached is presented, the application is, by a law so universal that it almost has acquired the nature of a landmark, referred to a committee of investigation, or, as it is often called, a committee on character.

The importance, and indeed the absolute necessity, of a proper and careful inquiry into the character of candidates for initiation cannot be too often or too deeply impressed upon the mind. It is the greatest of all the guards that the wisdom of our predecessors has thrown like ramparts around the security and safety of our Order.

So important has this preliminary step towards initiation been deemed, that the "General Regulations," approved in the year 1721, prescribe it as a positive law that "No man can be accepted a member of a particular Lodge, without previous notice one month before given to the Lodge, in order to make due inquiry into the reputation and capacity of the candidate, unless by dispensation."

This ancient regulation has, perhaps on account of its evident importance to the safety of the Institution, been better observed than any other of the old landmarks. While the contemporaneous rules in relation to the exclusion of maimed candidates, to the absence of religious tests, and many more of equally positive enactment, have from time to time been neglected or denied, I know of no Grand Lodge that has thought proper to abolish the "due inquiry" into character. The Grand Lodge of Virginia did, it is true, some years ago, propose to abolish committees of investigation, and to constitute all the members of the Lodge a committee of the whole on the character of the applicant; but the opposition here was not to the investigation, but to the mode in which it was conducted.

We are then to inquire into the parliamentary form, which, in Masonic bodies, is adopted in the constitution of this committee; next, into the duties which it is required and expected to per-

17   N

form; and, lastly, into the mode in which its report is to be made and action to be taken thereon.

As soon as a petition for initiation or affiliation has been read, it must be referred to a committee for investigation into the character and qualification of the candidate. Sometimes this committee is appointed on a motion made by some member. But as in every Lodge there is, or ought to be, a rule requiring the submission of the petition to a committee, it is not essentially necessary that any such motion should be made. The presiding officer may of his own motion make the reference and appoint the committee.

The old regulation, already referred to, designates specifically the time during which the committee is to exercise the inquiry, and the nature of the inquiry that is to be made. In other words, it defines precisely the duties and functions of the committee, and this definition has been made the basis of all subsequent regulations by Grand Lodges on the subject.

As the old regulation prescribes that a previous notice of one month shall be given to the Lodge, it is to be inferred that during that month the committee should be engaged in its investigation, so that, having been appointed at one

regular meeting, it shall be in order for it to report at the next.   This time is prescribed, not
merely to afford the committee an ample opportunity for investigation, but that by the "previous
notice" every one who knows anything that is
unfavorable to the character of the applicant
may, by being advertised of his petition, be enabled to come forward and state his objections.
It is a sacred duty which every Mason owes to
his Order, that he should not wait until he is
asked for the information in his possession, but
that he should voluntarily, and without any so-
licitation, make known all that he thinks would
render the proposed candidate unworthy of initiation.   Every member of the Order should be,
in fact, a guardian watching at the portals of the
Temple, to see that none pass into the sanctuary
but "he who has clean hands and a pure heart."

We are next to inquire what are the functions
to be discharged by the committee during this
interval of a month between the time of its appointment and that of its report, or, in other
words, what is the nature of the investigation
that has been committed to it.   Now, the old
regulation says that the inquiry is made that
the "reputation and capacity" of the candidate
may be discovered.   There is, then, a twofold

object in the investigation. The one as relates to his reputation, the other as to his capacity. The reputation of the candidate will affect the standing and character of the Institution into which he applies for admission, for good or for evil, accordingly as he shall be found worthy or unworthy of the favor that has been bestowed upon him. He must be "under the tongue of good report," and the Lodge which should admit a member without this indispensable qualification, would be bringing into our fold, not a lamb, the emblem of innocence and purity, but a ravenous wolf, who will inevitably destroy the flock.

But it is not simply into the reputation of the candidate that inquiry is to be made: his "capacity" presents also a subject of investigation. By the capacity of the candidate we understand his fitness to receive and to comprehend our sublime mysteries. According to the unwritten law of the Order, a fool or an idiot, an old man in his dotage, or a young one under age, is considered as an improper applicant for initiation, because, in these instances, there is either a total want of mind or an impaired or undeveloped intellect, which would render it impossible for the party initiated properly to appreciate the moral and philosophic instructions imparted to him.

Hence, the Grand Lodge of England, in view of this mental capacity, has provided in its regulations that the candidate "should be a lover of the liberal arts and sciences, and have made some progress in one or other of them."

These two distinctions of the "reputation" and the "capacity" of the candidate are alluded to in what is technically called the "investiture," or the presentation of the lambskin apron, which the neophyte is told to wear "with pleasure to himself and honor to the Fraternity." The pleasure to himself must depend on his *capacity* to appreciate and enjoy the symbolic instruction of the Institution; the honor to the Fraternity will result from the *reputation* which he may bring to the support of the Order.

Our next inquiry is into the mode in which the report is to be made, and the action to be taken thereon. And here it may be observed, that the report of this committee stands on a different footing from that of any other committee. The law, or at least the usage, of Masonry has prescribed a particular process through which candidates must pass before they can obtain a right to initiation or affiliation. Of this process the appointment of a committee, and the investigation and report of that committee within a

17 *

specified time, form integral parts. As no motion could be entertained, when the petition was
first read, to lay it on the table, or to postpone
its consideration, or to dispose of it in any other
form than by reference to a committee, so when
the month appropriated by the law to the investigation of character has passed, and the committee comes up to make its report, it is not, I
conceive, in order to make any motion for the
postponement of the report, which must as a
matter of course be received. If it were in order
to move its postponement, it would be in order
to move its postponement definitely or indefinitely. But to postpone the reception of the
report indefinitely would be equal to a withdrawal of the petition, which the concurring opinion of all Masonic jurists has decided cannot be
done; and so that which it is unlawful to do
directly might be accomplished in an indirect
way.

The time, then, having arrived for the report
to be made — that is to say, the regular meeting
immediately succeeding the one at which the petition had been read and referred — the report
is called up by the presiding officer in the regular
order of unfinished business. The chairman, or
some member of the committee, rises in his seat

and makes the report, or, as is more usual, the report is sent to the Secretary's desk, and read by
that officer.   And here occurs the only contin-
gency in which the report may be postponed; for
the committee, if it finds the duty of investigation
more difficult than had been expected, may ask
for further time, which will generally be granted,
until the next regular meeting; but if the committee has completed its inquiries, the report
will then be read.   The committee is not necessarily confined to any precise formula of language, and may or may not give its reasons for
the opinion at which it has arrived.   But this
opinion must be definitely expressed, as being
favorable or unfavorable to the petition.

The report of any other committee having
been read, the action of the Lodge which follows
would be either for its adoption, its rejection, to
lay it on the table, to postpone it, or to make
some other parliamentary disposition of it; but
none of these rules are applicable to the report
of a committee on character.   Here the ancient
and uninterrupted usage of the Order requires
that the action of the Lodge on such a report
must take the form of a ballot on the petition.
The presiding officer, as soon as the favorable
report is read, will order the ballot to be taken,

and the result declared.   There can be no discussion on the nature of the report or the character of the applicant ; but the ballot must immediately follow the reading of the report.

But the report may be unfavorable; and in
prescribing what action is then to be taken, we
are embarrassed by the fact that Masonic jurists
here materially differ in their views.   Some contend that an unfavorable report requires a ballot
just as much as a favorable one, and that there
is no mode of rejecting a candidate except by
the ballot.   But other jurists of equal reputation
contend that an unfavorable report is equal to a
rejection without a ballot, and in that case the
ballot should be dispensed with.   I confess that
I have always entertained the latter opinion, and
that if the report of the committee is unfavorable, the candidate is at once rejected without
ballot.   This usage is founded on the principles
of common sense ; for as one black ball is sufficient to reject an application, the unfavorable
report of a committee must necessarily and by
consequence include two unfavorable votes at
least.   It is therefore unnecessary to go into a ballot after such a report, since it is to be taken for
granted that the brethren who reported unfavor-
ably would, on a resort to the ballot, cast their

negative votes.   Their report is indeed virtually considered as the casting of such votes, and the applicant is therefore at once rejected without a further and unnecessary ballot.

Let us suppose that the other rule is the correct one, and that a ballot must be taken on an unfavorable report.   Now, it might be possible that when the ballot was taken, the members of the committee would be absent from the Lodge. The ballot might then also be clear, and thus a candidate would be elected in the face of the declaration of three members that he was unworthy, and who, if not prevented by circumstances, would have been present and would have deposited black balls.   It cannot be denied that such a proceeding would be worse than a farce, because it would be a violation of the entire spirit of the Masonic system in reference to the election of candidates.

It will be proper, in conclusion, to say something of the proper method in which the members of the committee should discharge the duty confided to them, and the form of the report which they should make.

Of all the committees appointed for the convenience of business by a Lodge, there is none so important as that to which has been consigned the duty of investigating the character of a petitioner for initiation.   It is always unfortunate for the interest of Masonry when such a committee is either ignorant of the responsibility of the task imposed on it or is careless in performing it. When an architect is appointed to superintend the construction of a building, he will, if honest and capable, inspect with the utmost care the character of every piece of material that the builders propose to use.   He will make no superficial examination, nor rest satisfied with the general appearance of the stone or timber that is submitted to his inspection.   He will, by a thorough and minute scrutiny, assure himself that the materials are of good quality, that they have been properly prepared, and that they will secure strength and stability to the edifice.   He does all this because he knows that if, when the structure is completed, it should prove weak and imperfect, his professional reputation would be impaired; and that if any fatal accident should result from this weakness or imperfection, he would be held morally, and perhaps legally, responsible for the consequences of such disaster.

Now, if the Lodge is, as our symbolism teaches us, the spiritual antitype of a material temple, of which every member constitutes a stone, and if in that temple it is required that none but perfect stones should be admitted, then it follows, in pursuance of the same symbolic idea, that the making of new Masons is the building up of the temple.   And in the process of this construction the members of the committee on character are the architects who are to judge of the quality of the material that is brought up, and they must pursue the same rule of caution and diligence that the professional architect would in supervising a material temple.

When the builder presents a stone that has been made ready for the building, the architect does not say, "I have heard no one say anything against this stone; nobody has told me that it is unfit material; you may deposit it in its designated place," but he examines it for himself; he applies to it the touchstone of his own professional knowledge; he says, "this is not granite, but sandstone; it is too soft and crumbling; if we use it, the wall would be weak."   Or he tries it with the plumb and square and level, and declares "it is too long; it must be made shorter;" or "its angles are not square, and its sides not perpendicular; it will not do."   And thus he rejects the material as unfit for use.   Or, if the inspection has satisfied him, he says, almost in the language of our own ritual: "This is good work, true work, square work, such work as we are authorized to receive," and the stone is then placed in the wall, and the building gains strength from the addition.

So, too, the committee on character, when a candidate is submitted to their inspection, must pursue the same cautious and prudent course in determining whether he is or is not a stone fit for the spiritual temple. In making up their report, they must not be content to say: "We have heard nothing against this candidate; no one has come to us accusing him of crime; we therefore recommend him for admission." Such a recommendation is based on negative information, or, to speak more correctly, has no basis at all, because no information has been received. The Lodge demands for its own security something more. It does not need to know only what evil has not been said of the candidate, but also what good has been said of him. General reputation is not sufficient. Each member of the committee should inquire for himself, not merely whether the candidate bears a good character in the community wherein he lives, for men too often seem to be what they are not, but what is his occupation, reputable or infamous? his habits, his intelligence, his disposition, his private as well as his public walk, and on this, and any additional information like this derived from such an inquiry, they should found their report.

The brief and unsatisfactory reports, too often made by these committees, are in language like this: "We recommend the candidate for initiation." On such a report, which really gives no information, the members are called upon to cast the ballot, and trusting to the fallacious hope that the committee has done its duty, they vote white balls, and thus too often ignorantly introduce a very bad stone into the temple.

But let us suppose that the committee, after strict inquiry, were to make a report something like this: "We find that the candidate is an industrious mechanic; that he honestly and respectably supports his family by his daily labor; that he is distinguished by an amiable disposition and gentle manners; that he is temperate in his habits and upright in his dealings; that he is a tender husband, an affectionate father, a faithful friend, and possessor of the amount of intelligence and intellectual culture that will enable him to comprehend and value the teachings of our Institution."

Or again: suppose, unfortunately for the
18

aspirant, the committee should report thus
" We find that the candidate is a professional
gambler, of intemperate habits, of coarse manners, of belligerent disposition, and of so low a
grade of intellect that if admitted he could neither
understand nor properly appreciate the lessons
of our ritual."

In each of these supposed cases the members
of the Lodge would find no difficulty in making
a right decision.   In the former case, good material would be accepted ; in the latter, worthless
would be rejected.

But it may be said that the inquiries which
must be instituted and pursued to enable the
committee to make such a report would involve
too much time and labor.   The objection is
worthless.   If in a Lodge of forty or fifty members — few have less, and many have more —
three men cannot be found who, with a month
to do it in, can divide the labor of such an inquiry between them, then it were better that
such a Lodge should close its doors to all admis-
sions, and remain content with its original membership.   Better not grow at all than to grow by
the accretion of bad materials.   " Ill weeds grow
apace," says the proverb.   But Lodges should
not be like ill weeds, but rather like salutiferous

plants, whose growth, though slow, will end in the production of wholesome fruit.

Reform on this subject is undoubtedly needed ; and, as a step towards it, it is recommended that the committee on character, to which a petition on initiation is referred, should be supplied with a form in which the following heads should be printed, the blanks to be filled as fully as possible by the committee :

"REPORT ON THE PETITION OF

"We find the following facts in reference to the applicant :

"Age. ——.

"Place of nativity.

"Occupation. ——.

"Habit of life. (*Sober, industrious, or otherwise.*)

"Manners. (*Pleasant and agreeable, or rude and boisterous, etc.*)

"Disposition. (*Amiable, gentle, or otherwise.*)

"Married or single. ——.

"Domestic relations. (*Conduct as a husband, father, friend, etc.*)

"Associations. (*With reputable people or with low characters.*)

"Amount of intelligence or intellectual culture.

"Miscellaneous.   (*Anything else that they may know of him.*)"

With such a report before it, no Lodge could err in coming to a conclusion on the important question of admitting a new member into the great family of which it constituted a part. I am sure that if this, or some similar form, were once adopted, no further complaint would be made, as is now too often done, of the carelessness or inefficiency of committees on character. A month might not be always a sufficient time in which to obtain the information thus required. If not, let there be no hurry; the committee should have further time. It is better that the candidate should wait a year than that the Lodge should make a mistake.

CHAPTER XXXIII.

OF FILLING BLANKS.

A PROPOSITION is sometimes presented to a meeting, and even adopted in an incomplete form; as when, in a motion for an appropriation for money, the precise amount is not stated; or when in a proposition to do something at a future time, the exact day is left for subsequent consideration. In each of these cases a blank occurs, which must be filled up. It is usual to leave the filling up of the blank until the motion is adopted, because, if it should be rejected, any further discussion of the subject would be unnecessary.

After the proposition has been adopted, the next question to be put by the chair is, "How shall the blank be filled?" And then, as the motion to fill the blank is not considered in the light of an amendment to the original motion, but rather as an independent proposition, which is intended to give it completion, any number of these propositions may be made. But of course there must be an order in which they are to be considered.

In the early days of the British Parliament, these blanks generally referred to the amount of taxes to be levied and to the time at which they should be collected. And as the object of the members was to reduce as much as possible the burdens of the people, the effort was always made to fill the blank for money with the smallest sum, and the blank for the day on which it was to be collected with the longest time. Hence sprang the rule, which still exists in Parliament, that in filling blanks the smallest sum and the longest time shall be first put.*

But in this country a different rule prevails. Here the reason that governs is not to begin at that extreme which and more, being, as Jefferson, citing Grey, says, within every man's wish, no one could negative it; and yet, if he should vote in the affirmative, every question for more would be precluded; but at the extreme which would unite few, and then to advance or recede until you get a number which will unite a bare majority. Hence the rule in the Congress of the United States, which has been universally adopted in all public meetings in this country, is to

* See Hatsell, Prec., iii. 184.

begin with the highest sum and the longest time ; and therefore the presiding officer will continue putting the propositions for filling the blank in this order, until the assembly comes to one on which a majority of the members can agree.

Sometimes the sum or time will be inserted by the mover in the original motion, so that no blank occurs. Yet as the sum or time proposed may not be satisfactory to all, an effort may be made to change it. But this can only be done in the form of an amendment, by moving to strike out and insert, and here the rule of the largest sum or the longest time will not prevail, but the parliamentary law of amendment will be in force. One amendment only, and one amendment to it, is permissible, and the latter must be put to the question first. Thus the original motion may be "to appoint a committee of *three* persons." An amendment may be offered to strike out *three* and insert *five ;* and this may again be amended by a motion to insert *seven* instead of *five.* The motion to *strike out and insert* may be divided. If the motion to *strike out* be lost, the motion to insert cannot be put, but a new motion may be made to *strike out three* and insert *nine,* or some number other than *five* or *seven.* If the motion to strike out be

adopted, then the amendment to insert *seven* will
be put in order; and, that being lost, then the
question will recur on inserting *five*.   If this also
be lost, the proposition will remain incomplete,
because *three* has been stricken out and nothing
inserted in its place, and a new amendment must
be offered for the insertion of some other number.   And the proceedings will continue by the
introduction of new figures, until the original
proposition is perfected by the adoption of some
number which will be satisfactory to the majority.

CHAPTER XXXIV.

OF CO-EXISTING QUESTIONS.

I T is a principle of parliamentary law that two independent propositions cannot be at the same time before a meeting. But during the pendency of a main question, a privileged motion may be made and entertained, and then these two motions, the original and the privileged one, constitute what are called co-existing questions. Now, it may be asked what becomes of the original motion, if the privileged one be decided in the affirmative. The answer will depend on the nature of the privileged motion that has been adopted. The parliamentary law prescribes that when a motion for adjournment is made and carried during the pendency of a question, that question is suppressed, and cannot again at a subsequent meeting be revived except by a new motion. As the closing of the Lodge is in Masonic usage equivalent to an adjournment, it is evident that the closing of the Lodge during the pendency of any question must have the same effect. But the inconvenience, and oftentimes the injustice, that would result from the rigid enforcement of such a rule has led to the adoption by Congress of a special regulation, by which such interrupted propositions are considered not as totally suppressed, but only as thrown into the class of unfinished business, to be taken up at the proper time, when such unfinished business would be in order. And although no such special regulation should be found in the rules of order of a Lodge, the spirit of comity and the dictates of convenience will always prevail ; and hence a question interrupted by the closing of the Lodge is only suppressed for the time, and will be renewed at the next communication as unfinished business.

So, during the pendency of any discussion, if the hour for any special order has arrived and that order is taken up, the pending question is suppressed for the time, but will be *ipso facto* renewed when the special order has been disposed of.

The pending question is also affected by some other motions, which are to lay on the table, to postpone indefinitely, to postpone to a certain time, or to commit ; all of which may co-exist with it, and must be taken up in the order of their precedence as privileged questions.

If all these motions are rejected, the discussion of the original proposition of course goes on. But if any one of them is adopted, the effect will be various. If the proposition is laid on the table, it is suppressed until called up again; if postponed indefinitely, it is permanently suppressed; if it be postponed to a certain time, it becomes a special order, and at that time takes precedence of all other motions; when it is committed, it can only be renewed by the report of the committee to which it has been committed.

CHAPTER XXXV.

OF THE DIVISION OF THE QUESTION.

IT is a well-settled principle of parliamentary law, that when a question contains more parts than one it may be divided into two or more questions. But to be thus divisible, the question must contain independent propositions so distinct and entire that one of them being taken away, the other may stand perfect and complete. For if, by the striking out of one of the propositions, the other will become meaningless, the question cannot be divided. The division of a question must be so made that each clause can stand by itself. Thus, a motion to appropriate money for the relief of a member is not divisible, because, if the clause "to appropriate money" be stricken out, the clause "for the relief of a member" would be without meaning. The congressional rule is very explicit, that the question may be divided "if it comprehends propositions in substance so distinct that one being taken away, a substantive proposition shall remain for the decision of the House."

By the parliamentary law of the English Commons, the House must decide whether a question is or is not divisible. But the rules of the American Senate and House of Representatives say that, "any member may call for the division of the question," but as it is subsequently provided that the division may be made if the question comprehends propositions that are substantially distinct, it would necessarily follow that the Speaker, and of course the House, may overrule the demand for a division, on the ground that the question does not comprehend distinct propositions, and, therefore is not divisible. Such is the usual practice in popular assemblies, and the same rule affects Masonic Lodges. Any member may call for a division of the question. If the presiding officer overrules the call, the division cannot be made, because there is no appeal from his decision. If any other member objects, the point must be settled by a vote of the Lodge. But if the call for a division is not overruled by the chair, or no objection is made, the proposition will be divided, and the question be put on each clause separately.

The call for a division of the question may be

19

made at any time before the vote is taken on the main question. The rules that prevail on this subject in the government of Masonic bodies may be briefly stated as follows:

1. Any member may, at any time before the vote is taken, demand a division of the question.

2. The presiding officer may overrule the demand because in his opinion the question is not capable of an intelligent division, and this puts an end to the matter.

3. Any member may object to the demand, and then the motion, whether the question shall be divided must be put to the Lodge.

4. If the demand is not overruled by the presiding officer, and no objection is made, the question will be divided, and each clause of the division will then be treated as a separate and independent question.

5. Neither clause so divided is subject to any of the subsidiary motions, except amendment. It may be amended, but it cannot be laid on the table or postponed. The question must be direct on its adoption.

CHAPTER XXXVI.

OF AMENDMENTS TO THE BY-LAWS.

THOSE rules which regulate and define the duties and privileges of its members in a Grand Lodge are called the *Constitution*, and in a Subordinate Lodge the *By-Laws*. What Mr. Rawle remarks of political constitutions may be just as well applied to those of private societies. He says:

" On the voluntary association of men in sufficient numbers to form a political community, the first step to be taken for their own security and happiness is to agree on the terms on which they are to be united and to act. They form a constitution or plan of government suited to their character, their exigencies, and their future prospects. They agree that it shall be the supreme rule of obligation among them." *

An essential element of this instrument is its permanency, at least so far as that no change can be made without due notice, so that the

* View of the Constitution of the United States, p. 5.

members may not be taken by surprise, by the
sudden enactment or repeal of a law.

Hence, in every constitution and code of by-
laws there is a provision by which embarrass-
ments are thrown in the way of change.   A simple resolution may be passed or be rescinded by
a bare majority vote; but to enact a new by-law,
or to repeal one that had been already enacted,
requires the affirmative vote of sometimes two-
thirds and sometimes three-fourths of the members present, and that, too, only after a previous
notice given one or two meetings before and
after two to three readings.

Now, the provision for the mode of this repeal
alteration, or amendment, is a part of every constitution or code of by-laws, and by that provision the Lodge and the presiding officer are to
be governed in the premises.

If the by-laws of a Lodge require that no alteration shall be made unless it be proposed in
writing at a regular communication, laid over
until the next regular communication, then read
a second time and adopted by the votes of two-
thirds of the members present, it is evident that
the duty of the presiding officer is to see that
these provisions are complied with, and they
themselves supply the necessary instructions for

his government. All that needs to be remarked is, that the amendment thus proposed takes the character of a special order, and as a privileged question has precedence of every other proposition when the time for action on it has arrived.

But it is necessary here to refer to one difficulty which is sometimes thrown in the way of a presiding officer, and which he should, by a proper knowledge of parliamentary law, be prepared to meet. And to understand this, it is most convenient to supply an example.

Let us suppose, then, that, with such a provision in the by-laws as that already cited, there is a clause which enacts that "the Lodge shall meet at 8 o'clock P. M. on the first Monday of every month." Now, an alteration may be proposed to strike out "first Monday" and insert "second Wednesday." This being proposed in writing, read at a regular communication, and recorded on the minutes, becomes the special order for the next regular communication; and, being then read a second time, will be adopted, if two-thirds of the members present concur. But when the proposition is before the Lodge for final action, some member may propose, as an amendment to this amendment, to strike out "Wednesday" and insert "Thursday." And it

19*

has been contended, that such an amendment to
the amendment could be submitted and be acted
on; but such a doctrine is altogether erroneous.
The original amendment was to change the time
of meeting from the "first Monday" to the
"second Wednesday," and this only can be
before the Lodge for consideration, since it alone
has gone through the regular and prescribed
form of two readings. The amendment to the
amendment, which would make, if adopted, an
alteration from the "first Monday" to the "second Thursday," has not been proposed at a
previous communication, has not been laid over,
and has not passed through a second reading.
Not having come before the Lodge in accordance
with the forms provided in the by-laws for alterations or amendments, it would be out of order
for the presiding officer to entertain it.

In other words, it may be laid down as a
rule, that no repeal, alteration, or amendment of
the by-laws having been proposed, can, at any
future time in the proceedings, be subjected to
change or amendment. The proposed alteration must be presented for final action in the
very words in which it was originally proposed.
The proper time for offering the amendment to
the amendment would be when the former was

first proposed. Both the amendment and the rider to it would thus go through the regular course, and both would come up for a second reading, and for action at the subsequent meeting. It is scarcely necessary to say, that in that case the amendment to the amendment would be first in order of consideration.

It has been contended that at the time of acting on a proposed amendment, a change in phraseology so as to improve the language, but which does not affect the spirit and meaning of the proposed amendment, is admissible. But as it is not always easy to determine whether the change in language may not alter the precise meaning, it is better to adhere to the strict rule, which permits no change to be made, but requires that the proposition shall be submitted to a vote in its original form.

It is admitted that no change in the by-laws of a Lodge can become operative until approved and confirmed by the Grand Lodge. But an inexperienced Master will sometimes permit a motion for the temporary suspension of a by-law, believing that such suspension may be made by unanimous consent; but such a proceeding is in violation of Masonic law. If a Lodge cannot re-

peal any one of its by-laws without the consent
of the Grand Lodge, it is an evident consequence
that it cannot suspend it; for this is, for all practical purposes, a repeal for a definite, although
temporary, period. It is the duty, therefore, of
the presiding officer to rule any proposition for
a suspension of a by-law to be out of order, and
therefore not admissible.

CHAPTER XXXVII.

OF NOMINATIONS TO OFFICE.

THE subject of nominations to office is germane to a treatise on the parliamentary law of Masonry, because the propriety and legality of such nominations has been made a question in some quarters, and therefore it becomes the duty of the presiding officer, if such a nomination is made, to decide whether it is or is not in order.

If there be no special regulation in the constitution of a Grand Lodge, or in the by-laws of a Subordinate Lodge, which forbids nominations for office, then such nominations are in order; for nomination is the Masonic rule and usage, and the neglect of it the exception.

The oldest record, after the Revival, that we have, informs us that on June 24, 1717, "before dinner, the oldest Master Mason (now the Master of a Lodge) in the chair *proposed a list of proper candidates;* and the brethren, by a major-

P   225

ity of hands, elected Mr. Anthony Sayre, gent., Grand Master of Masons." *

All the subsequent records of the Grand Lodge of England show an uninterrupted continuance of the custom, it being for a long time usual for the Grand Master to nominate his successor. The present constitution of that Grand Lodge requires that "the Grand Master shall, according to an ancient usage, be nominated at the quarterly communication in December." The custom of nomination is practised in some of the English Lodges, but discontinued in others; and Dr. Oliver, in his Jurisprudence, thinks it a practice that is open to objection, because there are, he says, few brethren who would be willing to incur the odium of voting against one who had been nominated. But while disapproving of a nomination on the ground of policy, he does not deny its legality.

If, therefore, there be no regulation of a Grand Lodge or of a Subordinate Lodge, which specifically prohibits nominations for office, such nominations will be in order, and must, when they are made, be entertained by the presiding officer.

* Anderson's Constitutions, 2d ed., p. 109.

CHAPTER XXXVIII.

THE first thing in order, after the ritual ceremonies of opening have been performed, is the reading and confirmation of the minutes, and the only question to be here considered is the limit that is to be made to proposed amendments or alterations of them ; for it is the duty of the Master, after the minutes have been read for the information of the Lodge, to inquire, first of the Wardens and then of the brethren, whether they have any alterations or amendments to suggest.

Now, it has sometimes been supposed that if any business has been transacted at the previous meeting of which the minutes purport to be a record, which it is desired to rescind or repeal, the proper method will be to propose an alteration of the minutes before confirmation, by which all reference to such business will be stricken out. But this evidently is an erroneous interpretation of the law, which proceeds from a misunderstanding of the true character of the minutes.

The minutes of a Lodge are supposed to be, and ought always to be, "a just and true record of all things proper to be written." They constitute the journal of the proceedings of the meeting to which they refer, as those proceedings actually occurred. If altered by the expurgation of any part, they cease to be a record.

It has occurred in the proceedings of the English Parliament and the American Congress that portions of the journal which contained the record of transactions which had become obnoxious, have been expunged by a vote taken subsequent to their confirmation; and these precedents, it is supposed, would authorize a Lodge to rescind or annul, or even to expunge, from its minutes any particular portion.

But the question on so rescinding, annulling, or expunging must be made after the minutes have been confirmed. The first question, and the only question in order after the minutes have been read, is, "Shall the minutes be confirmed?" And this question is simply equivalent to this other one: "Is it the sense of the Lodge that the Secretary has kept a just and true record of the proceedings." And the alterations or amendments to be suggested before this question is put, are not to change the record of what has really occurred, but to make the record just and true.

The decision has been made in Congress that "when a member's vote is *incorrectly* recorded, it is his right on the next day, while the journal is before the House for its approval, to have the journal corrected accordingly. But it is not in order to change a *correct record* of a vote given under a misapprehension."

In the Grand Lodge of England, the usage has been, when the question is on the confirmation of the minutes of a previous communication, to entertain a motion for the non-confirmation of the record of any resolution, the effect of which is to rescind the action of the preceding Grand Lodge. Sometimes the motion has been made to confirm one part of a resolution which had been adopted, and not to confirm the other part. This irregularity was so apparent, that in 1859, the Earl of Zetland, who was then Grand Master, declared that such a motion would be out of order. He admitted, however, the right of the Grand Lodge to refuse to confirm the minutes in reference to an individual resolution, although it was not denied that the record was correct.

20

This usage is so incorrect, that it is not surprising that the Earl of Zetland, in announcing his decision, should have declared that the practice in the Grand Lodge was so little analogous to that pursued in Parliament, that he could, in making up his opinion, "derive no assistance from parliamentary usage." Neither is it surprising that an intelligent writer in the "Freemasons' Magazine" for September, 1858, should have condemned what he calls this "piece of absurdity frequently performed in Grand Lodge."

"No one," he says, "can, when the minutes are correct, with any regard to truth, move that such minutes be not confirmed, nor can any amendment be entertained on the question that the minutes be confirmed which tends to alter or erase a minute correctly entered on the record."

This enounces the true principle. The question on confirmation of the minutes simply relates to the correctness of the record, and no motion or suggestion for an alteration can be made, except it be to correct a mistake or to supply an omission. The suggestion of any alteration which would affect the correctness of the record, would be out of order, and could not be entertained by the presiding officer.

Finally, as it is an accepted principle of Masonic law that the proceedings of a regular or stated communication cannot be reviewed or overruled at a special one, it follows that it is not competent at a special meeting to read, for confirmation, the minutes of the preceding regular communication.   Hence no minutes are read at special meetings, except perhaps at the close, for the information of the members, and for the correction of errors or for supplying omissions.   But the minutes can be read for confirmation only at a regular communication.

INDEX.

20 *

THE END.

The most Important Masonic Work ever Published.

ENCYCLOPÆDIA

OF

FREEMASONRY.

With Illustrations.

BY

ALBERT G. MACKEY, M. D.,

Author of "LEXICON OF FREEMASONRY," "A TEXT-BOOK
OF MASONIC JURISPRUDENCE," "SYMBOLISM
OF FREEMASONRY," Etc., Etc.

The work is printed in royal octavo, containing 960
pages, on fine paper, and in beautiful clear type, cast especially for this book. Many of the articles are illustrated
with fine engravings. An admirable likeness of the author,
engraved by John Sartain, embellishes the volume as a
frontispiece.

PRICE.

Handsomely bound in Cloth, Gilt Side.......... $9.00
Sheep, Library Style, Marble Edges............. 10.00
Half Morocco, Marble Edges...................... 11.00
Half Russia 11.00

Sold Exclusively by Subscription.

MOSS & CO.,

432 CHESTNUT STREET,
PHILADELPHIA.

21

"THE ENCYCLOPÆDIA OF FREE-MASONRY AND ITS COLLATERAL SCIENCES,"

By Albert G. Mackey, M.D., is the most learned and complete of any Masonic work ever written. It embraces articles on the RITUAL-ISM, JURISPRUDENCE, BIBLIOGRAPHY, BIOGRAPHY, HISTORY, LITERATURE, PHILOSOPHY, ETHICS AND SYMBOLISM OF THE ORDER.

The "Encyclopædia of Freemasonry" recommends itself to the patronage of the Fraternity for the following considerations:

1. There is no word used in Masonry of which the reader will not find a full explanation.

2. The history of the rise, the progress, and the present condition of Masonry, not only in every State and Territory of the UNITED STATES, but in every COUNTRY in the WORLD, is given under the appropriate head.

3. It contains an account of every Masonic writer who has ever existed, living ones excepted, and a full biographical sketch of the most distinguished, such as Oliver, Webb, Preston, Hutchinson, etc.

4. Every symbol is fully explained; its hidden as well as its commonly accepted meaning is given, its relation to other symbols, and the history of its origin and adoption as a symbol are treated in the most exhaustive manner. The Mason who attentively reads this work cannot fail to be an accomplished master of the science of Masonic symbolism.

2

5. Every Rite in Masonry is described. The history of its origin, the time and place when it was instituted, the name of the inventor, the peculiar character of the Rite, the number and names of the degrees of which it is composed, and its progress to the present day, or, if obsolete, the time and mode of its decay, are given in the fullest manner.

6. Over four hundred Masonic degrees are described, and of these the most important are treated in an exhaustive manner; the history of their origin, their object and design, and portions of their ritual are given.

7. The Legends and Myths of Freemasonry, a knowledge of which is so important to the Masonic student, are all fully detailed. Without an acquaintance with these legends, it would be impossible to comprehend correctly the true character of Speculative Masonry. They have for the first time been collected together in this work.

8. The subject of Masonic jurisprudence has been carefully treated. Every possible question of Masonic law has been discussed, and by reference to the appropriate articles, the reader may make himself acquainted with all questions relative to the rights, prerogatives, and duties of Lodges, Chapters, Councils, and their candidates and officers. For example, under the article "Suspension," the law on that subject will be found clearly enunciated. So also of "Crimes," "Punishments," and all other matters treated of in a book on Masonic jurisprudence.

9. The study of the Old Manuscript Constitutions of the Craft, written before the eighteenth century, most of which have been but recently discovered, has become absolutely necessary to a proper appreciation of the history of Masonry as a secret organization. Of every one of these Manuscripts a full account is given in the Encyclopædia. Not one has

been omitted, and hence this work becomes essentially necessary to any one who would desire to become acquainted with this interesting part of Masonic history.

10. There is no part of this work more interesting to the general scholar as well as to the Mason, than those articles which give a history of the ancient Mysteries and of the secret societies of the Middle Ages. The close connection in design between these associations and Freemasonry has made it necessary that they should be thoroughly understood by the Masonic scholar. There is no other work extant in which their history is embraced under one cover. The student would have to look for it elsewhere in many works, most of them of difficult access, from their rarity or costliness.

11. In short, there is no subject interesting to the Freemason, whether it be the religious bearing, the ritual, the history, the philosophy, the law, or the symbolism of the Institution, that is not treated in the more than 4,000 articles of this extensive dictionary. It will supply the place to all, except those who would study Masonry as authors, of a costly and extensive library. With this book in his possession, the Mason may devote a few hours from time to time to its perusal, and at the close of his reading will be better versed in all that is connected with the Order than nine-tenths of those who have not had the advantage of this compact, yet extensive source of instruction.

NOTICES OF THE PRESS.

Philadelphia Keystone.

"Mackey's Encyclopædia of Freemasonry" is the latest, and ranks with the very best, of modern works upon the art, science, and handicraft of Masonry. It is an original work ; not a bare compilation. Dr. Mackey is an authority on Masonry; his sentences are never slipshod, nor his opinions shallow. Had he indeed chosen to be a mere compiler, he could have gathered from his own voluminous writings, without consulting others, materials to fill as ample a volume as the present one ; that, however, has not been his aim. Every brother who has been "brought to *light*," and desires to live in the light, should own this volume, and have it handy continually for reference.

Forney's Press, Philadelphia.

Up to the present time the modern literature of Freemasonry has been diffuse and unreliable. Of course, this one volume will supersede the lumbering fifty volumes written by Dr. Oliver, whose works are not accepted as orthodox or accurate by well-informed members of the Order. Those who bear in mind that the word Encyclopædia, derived from the Greek, means "a circle of instruction," need not be told that Dr. Mackey's great work tells everything that may be known about the Masonic Order, past and present.

Philadelphia Evening Telegraph.

A very important and valuable contribution to the literature of Freemasonry has been made by Dr. Albert G. Mackey. This is by all odds the most learned, elaborate, readable, and instructive work on Freemasonry we have ever met with ; and it is deserving of a place in every library that makes any pretension to completeness.

NOTICES OF THE PRESS.

Union Herald, Charleston, S. C.

Every intelligent Mason, and every Masonic library, should not fail to procure it. It comprises the result of more than thirty years of labor, study, and research, every line of which has been written by the distinguished author.

Masonic Jewel, Memphis, Tenn.

It is far superior to any work of the kind ever before published —the crown book of all of Mackey's publications—a Bible to Freemasonry. Not that we endorse Brother Mackey in all his views, or believe him correct in all his statements, but this book comes so near being a complete library on Masonry in itself, that we are disposed to give it our unqualified endorsement. The work is a very large one; the learning and research displayed therein is wonderful and exceeding thorough.

Harper's Weekly.

This book will be welcomed by Masonic students as the most valuable contribution which has appeared either in the United States or England. The work is the result of many years of patient research, investigation, and thoughtful study.

London (England) Freemason.

Brother Mackey's work has at last reached this country. It does not belie the great fame or high ability of our excellent American brother. It will be welcomed by all Masonic students as the most valuable contribution to Masonic archæology, history, and science which has yet appeared in the United States or Great Britain. Those who peruse it will find themselves amply rewarded for the expenditure of time and money. It is a work which ought to be in the library of every Lodge and of every Masonic student. Is most creditable to our brother, an honor to America, and destined, we believe, to advance the great and happy cause of Masonic literature.

6

NOTICES OF THE PRESS.

Willimantic Journal, Conn.

No member of the Order can be without it, if they desire to be thoroughly posted in the history and symbolism of the Fraternity.

Freemasons' Repository, Providence, R. I.

We have arisen from a careful examination of Mackey's Encyclopædia of Freemasonry with a feeling of profound gratitude to the author for the valuable contribution which he has made to the history, science, and literature of the Masonic institution. Instead of the crude and ill-expressed statements and opinions so common in too many works of the kind, the work exemplifies the fruits of extensive reading and scholarly research, embellished with the graces of rhetoric and the accompaniments of a pure classic style. No wonder he has attracted the attention of the learned. The fiat, " Let there be light," has gone forth. The printing-press is scattering on every hand the leaves of Masonic knowledge and culture.

The Freemason, St. Louis, Mo.

This splendid work will long stand — a grand monument to its author, of invaluable worth to the Craft. It is so far superior to any of his former efforts, and other Masonic dictionaries, that comparison is out of the question. It is almost impossible to think of any subject connected with secret societies cognate to Freemasonry which it does not fully define.

Sunday Dispatch, Philadelphia.

Here are to be found explanations frequently sought for by historical students, but difficult — almost impossible — to be obtained except by long research and knowledge of the sources of information from which alone the instruction required can be obtained. The work is much more than a Cyclopædia of Freemasonry. It is a cyclopædia of mythology, knighthood, religion, and of almost every curious fact connected with associations of men. It is a book which every Mason who takes an *interest* in the history and progress of his Order ought to have.

The Bulletin, Norwich, Conn.

The volume treats upon the order of Masonry from its foundation, giving a concise definition and history of all the symbols and grades of the Order proper to be placed on paper; a historical sketch of the ups and downs of the Order, its persecutions and martyrdoms, the life and services of all the principal members of the Order who, years ago, defied the whole world, and stood by the great lights and truths that are to be learned within the Lodge Room, and not only those of the dark days of Masonry, but of more modern times. A full description of the Crusaders is also to be found in its pages, with a history of the order of the Knights Templar. The book is one that will command the attention of all, and every person who is fortunate enough to possess a copy will be unwilling to part with it at any price.

Brethren, suffer a word of exhortation : procure a copy of this Encyclopædia; you will have occasion to refer to its ample pages again and again. The information you thus receive will enable you to comprehend intelligently all subjects pertaining to the Craft, and give a reason to yourself for the "hope that is within you."

Public Ledger, Philadelphia.

Probably the most complete and exhaustive Masonic work yet published is the Encyclopædia of Freemasonry and its Kindred Sciences, by Dr. Albert G. Mackey. Its preparation has involved a prodigious amount of labor and research. He has written other and smaller works on the subject; but in this one has gathered everything that can be obtained in the whole range of history and literature that sheds any light upon the extensive and powerful society to which he has devoted so much attention. *An index* is also added, which is of great use to the reader. The work itself is a fine specimen of typographic art, and is quite creditable to both printer and publisher.

The Argus, Port Townsend, W. T.

Every member, and every constituted body of every rite, ought to be the possessor of a copy of this work. It is the largest, finest, and most perfect compendium of Freemasonry ever published.

The Daily Oregonian, Portland, Oregon.

Matters connected with Freemasonry have been the study of Dr. Mackey's lifetime, and no man living is better qualified than he to write them.

London (England) Masonic Magazine.

All honor to Dr. Mackey for the zeal he has evinced and the sacrifices he must have made in the good cause of Masonic literature, and all praise to him, and gratitude from many a Masonic student, for the labor he has undergone, the skill he has employed, and the learning he displays in this his last and most striking literary production. It is the most clear, and condensed, and compact dictionary of Freemasonry now in existence, and a cursory perusal has convinced us how carefully Brother Mackey has collated all his authorities, verified his quotations, and how very able are his own personal editorship and contributions from first to last, of which he speaks, we observe, in such modest terms.

MASONIC CERTIFICATES.

FROM STEEL PLATES. — Original Designs.

Master Masons' Diplomas.
Size, 10x15 inches.

Bank Note Paper Sheets............ each, $		50
Bank Note Paper, Cloth Case, for Pocket................. "		75
Bristol Board Sheets, for Framing.................... "	1	00
Parchment Sheets, for Framing............................ "	1	00
Parchment, in Morocco Cases, for Pocket.......... .... "	1	50

Life Members' Certificates, for Master Masons.
Size, 10x15 inches.

Bank Note Paper, Sheets.........................each,		50
Bank Note Paper, Cloth Case, for Pocket.................. "		75
Bristol Board Sheets, for Framing. .... "	1	00
Parchment Sheets, for Framing.. .... "	1	00
Parchment, in Morocco Cases, for Pocket....... .... "	1	50

Master Mason's Widow's Certificate.
Size, 10x15 inches.

Bank Note Paper, Sheets.......... ....each,		50
Bank Note Paper, in Cloth Case, for Pocket.............. "		75
Bristol Board Sheets, for Framing............................ "	1	00
Parchment Sheets, for Framing............................... "	1	00
Parchment, in Morocco Cases, for Pocket.................. "	1	50

Master Masons' Demits, or Lodge Certificates.
Size, 15x18 inches.

Bank Note Paper, Sheets..................................each,	38
Bank Note Paper, in Cloth Case, for Pocket.............. "	50

Master Masons' Travelling Certificates.
Size, 15x18 inches.

Bank Note Paper, Sheets..................................each,	38
Bank Note Paper, in Cloth Case, for Pocket............ "	50

Master Mason's Diploma.
Size, 16x20 inches.

Bank Note Paper, Sheets............each, $		50
Bank Note Paper, in Cloth Case, for Pocket.............. "		75
Bristol Board Sheets, for Framing............ "	1	25
Parchment Sheets, for Framing............ "	1	25
Parchment in Morocco Tuck Case, for Pocket............ "	2	00

Royal Arch Diploma.
Size, 16x20 inches.

Bank Note Paper, Sheets............each,		50
Bank Note Paper, in Cloth Case, for Pocket.............. "		75
Bristol Board Sheets, for Framing............ "	1	25
Parchment Sheets, for Framing............ "	1	25
Parchment in Morocco Tuck Case, for Pocket............ "	2	00

Royal and Select Master's Diploma.
Size, 16x20 inches.

Bank Note Paper, Sheets............each,		50
Bank Note Paper, in Cloth Case, for Pocket.............. "		75
Bristol Board Sheets, for Framing............ "	1	25
Parchment Sheets, for Framing............ "	1	25
Parchment in Morocco Tuck Case, for Pocket............ "	2	00

Knights Templar Diploma.
Size, 16x20 inches.

Bank Note Paper, Sheets............each,		50
Bank Note Paper, in Cloth Case, for Pocket.............. "		75
Bristol Board Sheets, for Framing............ "	1	25
Parchment Sheets, for Framing............ "	1	25
Parchment in Morocco Tuck Case, for Pocket............ "	2	00

M. M., R. A., and K. T. Diploma.
On Parchment, bound together, Morocco Case, for Pocket, each, 5 00

M. M., R. A., R and S., and K. T. Diploma.
On Parchment, bound together, Morocco Case, for Pocket, each, 6 00

Sent on receipt of price to any address.

MOSS & CO., PUBLISHERS,
432 *Chestnut Street, Philadelphia.*

II

www.ingramcontent.com/pod-product-compliance
Lightning Source LLC
Chambersburg PA
CBHW060242290526
45789CB00001B/152